CONTENTS

HOW TO PASS THE DRIVER CPC

Harry Jones

HOW TO PASS THE DRIVER CPC

Harry Jones

FOREWORD

The Driver CPC is for LGV and PCV drivers who drive professionally throughout the UK. It has been developed as a requirement of the EU Directive 2003/59, which is designed to improve the knowledge and skills of professional LGV and PCV drivers throughout their working life. There are two parts to the legislation:

Part 1 - The Initial Qualification must be achieved by new LGV and PCV drivers along with their vocational licence to enable them to use their licence professionally.

Part 2 - Periodic Training; 35 hours of training every 5 years must be attended by all professional drivers

This manual is to give new and experienced drivers the knowledge and skills to pass the Driver CPC modules and perhaps more importantly, to fully understand the various aspects of the Driver CPC qualification so that studying for the test is made much easier. Harry Jones is an experienced author of a range or publications that are vital parts of current road transport legislation.

INTRODUCTION

The introduction of the Driver CPC is a radical step forward by Europe to standardise and improve the quality of commercial drivers across the continent. What we intend for this training manual is to simplify what can be a complicated and confusing process, enabling you to study it piece by piece and enter each module of the examinations with confidence that you will pass. Remember, much of the exam will be by multiple choice questions, the correct answer will be in front of you, a good preparation will enable you to instinctively understand and give the correct answer.

Subjects that the examinations focus on are:

- Vehicle controls, equipment and components
- Behaviour on the road
- Vehicle characteristics
- Load and weather conditions
- Traffic signs, rules and regulations
- Vehicle control and procedure
- Motorway driving
- Eco-safe driving
- Driving techniques
- Safe and Fuel-Efficient driving

- Load safety
- Securing of loads
- Types of loads
- Paperwork
- Vehicle maintenance
- The affects of alcohol
- Regulations governing the carriage of illegal immigrants
- Regulations that govern drivers' hours and tachographs
- Health and safety at work
- Driver health
- Dealing with emergencies
- The role of the driver within the company/organisation
- Freight transport organisation

Subsequent examinations are in a variety of ways, including multiple choice questions, interactive videos that need you to identify potential hazards etc., a practical test on the road as well as a test of your ability to load and unload your vehicle safely and correctly.

You will need an understanding of a range of ancillary subjects to do with health and safety, the environment and more.

It may sound confusing, but our mission here is to make it clear to you and equip you with the ability to pass each module first time.

SYLLABUS

SYLLABUS 1

Advanced Training in Rational Driving Based on Safety Regulations
All Licences

1.1
Objective: To know the characteristics of the transmission system in order to make the best possible use of it.
Curves relating to torque, power, and specific consumption of an engine, area of optimum use of revolution counter, gearbox-ratio cover diagrams.

1.2
Objective: To know the technical characteristics and operation of the safety controls in order to control the vehicle, minimise wear and tear and prevent disfunctioning.
Specific features of hydraulic vacuum servo-brake circuit, limits to the use of brakes and retarder, combined use of brakes and retarder, making better use of speed and gear ratio, making use of vehicle inertia, using ways of slowing down and braking on downhill stretches, action in the event of failure.

1.3
Objective: Ability to optimise fuel consumption.
Optimisation of fuel consumption by applying know how as regards points 1.1 and 1.2 (above).

Licences C, C+E, C1, C1+E

1.4
Objective: Ability to load the vehicle with due regard for safety rules and proper vehicle use.

Forces affecting vehicles in motion, use of gearbox-ratios according to vehicle load and road profile, calculation of payload of vehicle or assembly, calculation of total volume, load distribution, consequences of overloading the axle, vehicle stability and centre of gravity, types of packaging and pallets; main categories of goods needing securing, clamping and securing techniques, use of securing straps, checking of securing devices, use of handling equipment, placing and removal of tarpaulins.

Licences D, D+E, D1, D1+E

1.5
Objective: Ability to ensure passenger comfort and safety.
Adjusting longitudinal and sideways movements, road sharing, position on the road, smooth braking, overhang operation, using specific infrastructures (public areas, dedicated lanes), managing conflicts between safe driving and other roles as a driver, interacting with passengers, the needs of certain groups of passengers (disabled persons, children).

1.6

Objective: Ability to load the vehicle with due regard for safety rules and proper vehicle use.

Forces affecting vehicles in motion, use of gearbox ratios according to vehicle load and road profile, calculation of payload of vehicle or assembly, load distribution, consequences of overloading the axle, vehicle stability and centre of gravity.

SYLLABUS 2

Application of Regulations
All Licences

2.1

Objective : To know the social environment of road transport and the rules governing it.

Maximum working periods specific to the transport industry; principles, application and consequences of Regulations (EEC) 561/06 and 3821/85; penalties for failure to use, improper use of and tampering with the tachograph; knowledge of the social environment of road transport: rights and duties of drivers as regards initial qualification and periodic training.

Licences C, C+E, C1, C1+E

2.2

Objective: To know the regulations governing the carriage of goods.

Transport operating licences, obligations under standard contracts for the carriage of goods, drafting of documents which form the transport contract, international transport permits, obligations under the Convention on the Contract for the International Carriage of Goods by Road, drafting of the international consignment note, crossing borders, freight forwarders, special documents accompanying goods.

Licences D, D+E, D1, D1+E

2.3 Objective: To know the regulations governing the carriage of passengers.
Carriage of specific groups of passengers, safety equipment on board buses, safety belts, vehicle load.

SYLLABUS 3

Health, Road and Environmental Safety, Service, Logistics
All Licences

3.1
Objective: To make drivers aware of the risks of the road and of accidents at work.

Types of accidents at work in the transport sector, road accident statistics, involvement of lorries/coaches/buses, human, material and financial consequences.

3.2
Objective: Ability to prevent originality and trafficking in illegal immigrants.

General information, implications for drivers, preventive measures, check list, legislation on transport operator liability.

3.3
Objective: Ability to prevent physical risks.

Ergonomic principles; movements and postures which pose a risk, physical fitness, handling exercises, personal protection.
3.4
Objective: Awareness of the importance of physical and mental ability.

Principles of healthy, balanced eating, effects of alcohol, drugs or any other substance likely to affect behaviour, symptoms, causes, effects of fatigue and stress, fundamental role of the basic work/ rest cycle.

3.5
Objective: Ability to assess emergency situations.

Behaviour in an emergency situation: assessment of the situation, avoiding complications of an accident, summoning assistance, assisting casualties and giving first aid, reaction in the event of fire, evacuation of occupants of a lorry/bus/coach passengers, ensuring the safety of all passengers, reaction in the event of aggression; basic principles for the drafting of an accident report.

3.6
Objective: Ability to adopt behaviour to help enhance the image of the company.

Behaviour of the driver and company image: importance for the company of the standard of service provided by the driver, the roles of the driver, people with whom the driver will be dealing, vehicle maintenance, work organisation, commercial and financial

effects of a dispute.
Licences C, C+E, C1, C1+E

3.7
Objective: To know the economic environment of road haulage and the organisation of the market.

Road transport in relation to other modes of transport (competition, shippers), different road transport activities (transport for hire or reward, own account, auxiliary transport activities), organisation of the main types of transport company and auxiliary transport activities, different transport specialisations (road tanker, controlled temperature, etc.), changes in the industry (diversification of services provided, rail-road, subcontracting, etc.).

DRIVER CPC MODULES

MODULE 1 - THEORY AND HAZARD AWARENESS TEST

Module 1a consists of 100 multiple choice on-screen questions.
- A pass mark of 85 is required.
- Cost of this test is £35.00 (check for current rates).
- Candidates allowed 2 hours to complete this module.

Module 1b consists of 19 video clips containing 20 hazards (HPT - Hazard Perception Test)
- A pass mark of 67% is required
- Cost of this test is £15.00 (check for current rates).
- Candidates allowed ½ hr to complete this module.

If either test is failed then only that test needs to be retaken - not both.

Module 1 covers these subject areas:
- goods vehicle weights and dimensions
- secure load stowage and safe loading
- the polluting effects of excessive exhaust smoke
- legal markings on vehicles
- vehicle braking systems — types of brake and how they work

- maintenance and inspection of vehicle brakes
- correct use of heavy vehicle braking systems
- the risks and adverse effects of tailgating
- the effects of freezing weather conditions on vehicle braking systems
- how power steering systems work
- the law on speed limiters
- drivers' hours rules and rest period requirements
- legal requirements on record keeping
- the law on tachograph fitment and use of tachographs
- the effects of tiredness on drivers
- driver responsibility for the security of his vehicle and load
- stability of high and long vehicles
- the carriage and use of safety equipment
- how to reduce the risk of road accidents
- dealing with injuries;
- what to do if an accident involves hazardous materials
- how to deal with casualties
- reporting accidents
- carrying out safety checks, particularly on brakes, steering and tyres to ensure the vehicle is in a safe and legal condition
- understanding the legal requirements about vehicles being kept safe and roadworthy
- the effects of windy weather, particularly cross-winds, on high-sided vehicles
- the use of air deflectors to reduce wind resistance and improve fuel consumption
- the adverse effects of heavy rain causing excessive spray, which affects other road users and reduces the grip of tyres on wet roads

Module 2 - Case Studies for the Initial Driver Certificate of Professional Competence (IDCPC)

The Case Studies Test is optional if you only want to get a vocational licence and do not want to drive for a living. You must take it if you want to drive professionally and qualify for a full Driver Certificate of Professional Competence (Driver CPC).

The Case Studies Test is a computer-based exercise. You will be given seven case studies based on real-life situations you are likely to come across in your working life. Examples could be driving a bus in icy conditions or being asked to carry out non-driving work when you are due to take weekly or daily rest. The aim is to test your knowledge, and how you put it into practice. There will be seven case studies, each one with six to eight questions, with a possible maximum score of 50. The pass mark for the PCV test is 40 and the pass mark for the LGV test is 38. The test will take about one and a half hours to complete.

Module 3 - Practical Test (Module 1 must be passed before this test can be taken)

- Practical on-road driving test.
- Including an Eco-Safe Driving assessment - this will not contribute to the result of the test.
- Actual on-road driving time for all C (rigid) categories will be a minimum of 1 hour.

Test Criteria:
- Answer approximately 5 questions on basic vehicle checks.
- Reverse into a marked bay
- Controlled brake test.
- Test may also include hill starts and motorway driving.

You will need to have passed the part one theory test before you can take the practical test of driving ability for larger vehicles.

If you want to drive buses, coaches or lorries, you must pass the practical test before you can apply for a full vocational licence, regardless of whether or not you want to get a Driver Certificate of Professional Competence.

The test will take an hour and a half, with at least an hour of driving. The examiner will assess your driving in a variety of traffic conditions, and on several different types of road.

From 4 October 2010, the practical driving test includes approximately ten minutes of independent driving. This is designed to test your ability to drive unsupervised, and make safe decisions without guidance. Your practical driving test will include a ten-minute section of independent driving.

During your test you will have to drive independently by either following:

- traffic signs
- a series of direction
- a combination of both

Independent driving is not a test of your orientation and navigation skills, or your ability to remember directions. Driving independently means making your own decisions - this includes deciding when it is safe and appropriate to ask for confirmation about where you are going.

To help you understand where you are going, the examiner may show you a diagram.

If you go off the route or take a wrong turning, the examiner will help you to get back on the route and continue with the independent driving. Going off the driving route will not affect your result unless you commit a driving fault.

You will not need to have a detailed knowledge of the area. You cannot use a sat nav for independent driving as it gives you turn-by-turn prompts.

The practical test is made up of two parts.
The first is a reversing exercise, and is taken at the test centre.

The second takes place on public roads. It may include driving on motorways, depending on where you take your test. You will have to carry out exercises specific to the type of vehicle you drive. For example, if you are driving a bus or a coach, you will be asked to stop at a bus stop and move away when the examiner tells you to.

The practical test also includes an eco-safe driving assessment which involves the examiner taking note of how you control the vehicle and plan your driving. This assessment does not count towards the result of the test, however the examiner will give you feedback at the end of your test.

MODULE 4 - for the Initial Driver Certificate Of Professional Competence (IDCPC)

Module 2 must be passed before this test can be taken. This will be taken at the same test centre as Module 3.

It may be taken on the same day or a separate day.

During the test you will be required to demonstrate your knowledge and ability in the areas listed below:

• Ability to load the vehicle with due regard for safety rules and proper vehicle use.

- Security of the vehicle and contents.
- Ability to prevent criminality and trafficking in illegal immigrants.
- Ability to assess emergency situations.
- Ability to prevent physical risk.

Emphasis will be on you to demonstrate your ability e.g. through a physical walk-round vehicle safety check.

- The test consists of five questions which cover the Driver CPC syllabus.
- For each of the questions the examiner will require you to demonstrate your knowledge in the syllabus areas mentioned above, which could involve you carrying out actions such as walking round the vehicle pointing out relevant parts of a vehicle, or demonstrating the use of relevant parts of the vehicle.
- Each question equals 20% of the overall pass mark. To pass the test an overall score of 80% must be achieved, with a score of at least 15% in each question.

LGV tests will also see the introduction of a new piece of equipment called the 'Load Securing Demonstration Trolley' (LSDT) which will allow you to demonstrate your ability to secure loads using a variety of methods including ropes, chains, straps, etc.

Subsequently drivers need to undertake Periodic Driver CPC training for current LGV and PCV licence holders of

- bus (PCV) licence categories: D1, D1+E, D, D+E
- truck (LGV) licence categories: C1, C1+E, C, C+E

Current bus and truck drivers will need to do 5 days training every

5 years covering the following topics:

1. Advanced Training In Rational Driving Based On Safety Regulations.
2. Application of Regulations.
3. Health, Road and Environmental Safety, Service, Logistics.

A FEW FACTS ABOUT THE DRIVER CPC

A new qualification for professional lorry drivers - the Driver Certificate of Professional Competence (Driver CPC) - came into effect 10 September 2009 for lorry drivers. All professional LGV drivers are affected by this EU requirement to hold a Driver CPC. The Driver CPC is renewable every 5 years.

EU Directive 2003/59 requires all professional lorry drivers to hold a Driver CPC in addition to their vocational driving licence. For new drivers it introduces a new initial qualification which increases the amount of knowledge that drivers need before they can drive. When combined with the current licence acquisition tests, the initial qualification comprises a 4-hour theory test and a 2-hour practical test.

All drivers, new and existing, will then have to undertake 35 hours of training every 5 years to ensure that their Driver CPC is current. This is known as Periodic Training. Periodic Training is designed to confirm and expand on the existing knowledge and skills of each driver to ensure that they continue to be safe, courteous and fuel efficient drivers. This will also enable drivers to keep up-to-date with ever changing regulations and to benefit from training throughout their whole career.

All existing professional LGV drivers who held a full, valid category C, C1, C+E or C1+E licence at 10 September 2009 will need to complete the 35 hours of periodic training by 10 September 2014, unless they are exempt. This also includes drivers who hold C1 entitlement by virtue of passing a car test pre 1997. After this, they will need to undertake a further 35 hours of periodic training in every subsequent 5-year period in order to retain their Driver CPC. Existing LGV drivers are known as 'Acquired Rights' drivers i.e. drivers who already held a full vocational licence to drive lorries prior to 10 September 2009.

Driver CPC is short for Driver Certificate of Professional Competence. It is a new qualification that all professional bus, coach and lorry drivers, who need to have this qualification if they want to continue to drive professionally.

CPC affects all professional drivers of lorries over 3.5 tonnes, buses, coaches and minibuses with more than 8 passenger seats unless they qualify for an exemption.

You cannot work as a driver without a Driver CPC unless in exempted circumstances or you are following a National Vocational Training Scheme.

Exceptions from the Driver CPC qualification for Drivers of Vehicles

- used for non-commercial carriage of passengers or goods, for personal use
- undergoing road tests for technical development, repair or maintenance purposes, or of new or rebuilt vehicles which have not yet been put into service
- used in the course of driving lessons for the purpose of enabling that person to obtain a driving licence or a Driver CPC
- carrying material or equipment to be used by that person in the course of his or her work, provided that driving that

vehicle does not constitute the driver's principal activity*
- with a maximum authorised speed not exceeding 45 km/h
- used by, or under the control of, the armed forces, civil defence, the fire service and forces responsible for maintaining public order
- used in states of emergency or assigned to rescue missions

An example of a driver under exemption (also known as 'incidental driver') would be a bricklayer who drives a load of bricks from the builder's yard to the building site and then spends their working day laying bricks. In this case, driving a lorry is incidental to their main occupation.

A DQC is a card that is issued once the theory and practical tests of competence have been passed and or the relevant 'periodic training' is taken. These cards are issued for a 5 year period.

	Module	Price
1a	Theory Test - multiple choice questions	35
1b	Theory Test - hazard perception clips	15
2	Driver CPC Case Studies	30
3	Practical Driving Test	
	- weekdays	66
	- weekends and evenings	99
4	Driver CPC Practical Test (vehicle safety demonstration)	55

If you held a full, valid category D, D1, D+E, or D1+E PCV licence prior to 10th September 2008 or a full valid category C, C1, C+E, or C1+E LGV licence prior to 10th September 2009 you have 'acquired rights' which means you do not have to pass the initial qualification.

However, you are still required to complete periodic training every 5 years. This periodic training will consist of 35 hours of training to be taken over the 5-year period and will be in blocks of not less than 7 hours. Drivers with 'acquired rights' will be required to complete their first 35 hours of periodic training within the first 5 years following implementation of Driver CPC if they wish to continue to drive professionally.

New drivers, however, who pass their theory and practical driving test after the date of implementation of Driver CPC are required to complete a Driver CPC theory and practical test. The Driver CPC lasts for 5 years and drivers will need to complete 35 hours of periodic training every 5 years to retain their Driver CPC which entitles them to drive professionally.

The initial qualification has been divided into 4 modules to give you the flexibility to obtain your Category C/C1 or D/D1 licence only, or full Driver CPC, all at the same time.

The table below shows the different modules you will need to pass:

Module
1a   Theory Test - multiple choice questions
1b   Theory Test - hazard perception clips
2   Driver CPC Case Studies
3   Practical Driving Test
4   Driver CPC Practical Test (vehicle safety demonstration)

If you take your test after the Driver CPC start dates and you are not going to be driving for a living, you will only need to pass Modules 1 and 3. If, at a later date, you change your mind and want to drive for a living, you will need to pass Modules 2 and 4.

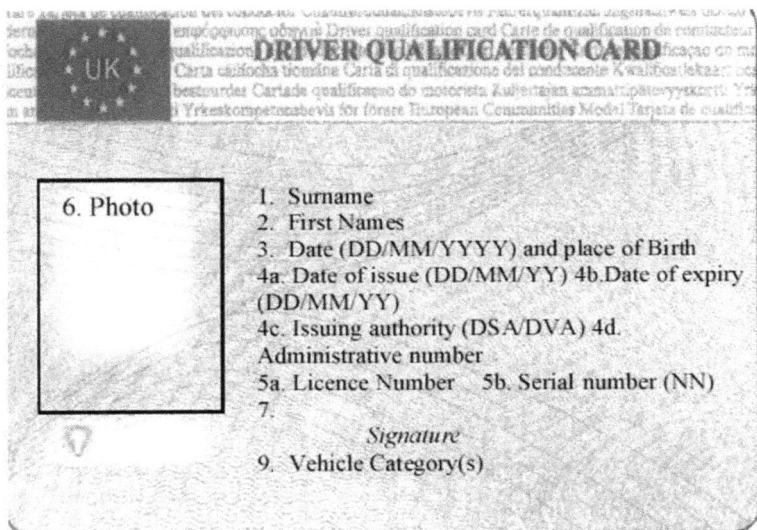

You must pass module 1 (a & b) before you can take module 3, and you must pass module 2 before you take module 4. In other words, the theory test must be passed before the practical part. However, you can take modules 2 and 4 before modules 1 and 3, or vice versa.

Drivers who already hold a Driver CPC for one category of vehicle (i.e. PCV or LGV) and wish to obtain a Driver CPC for the other category, will need to take a Module 2 conversion test consisting of 10 case studies with a total of 50 questions.

If a driver holds a Driver CPC for categories C or D they do not need a further one to draw a trailer for this category. This does not affect their requirement to pass the current driving test for the additional category.

The Case Studies Test is a computer based exercise. You will be given seven case studies based on real-life situations you arere likely to come across in your working life. The aim is to test your knowledge, and how you put it into practice. Each test is made up of seven case studies, each one with six to eight questions, with a possible maximum score of 50.

You can use the same vehicle for the practical driving test Module 3 and the Driver CPC Module 4.

You will need a full car driving licence and provisional entitlement for the category of test you wish to take (PCV or LGV).

PERIODIC TRAINING

All drivers, new and existing, will have to undertake a minimum of 35 hours of training every five years to ensure that their Driver CPC is current. This is known as Periodic Training. Periodic Training is designed to confirm and expand on existing knowledge and skills of each driver to ensure that they continue to be safe, courteous and fuel efficient drivers. This will enable drivers to keep up to date with ever changing regulations and to benefit from training throughout their whole career.

All drivers must undertake a minimum of 35 hours of training in every 5-year period. The minimum length of a training course that contributes to the Periodic Training requirement is seven hours.

Training is delivered by training centres that are approved by the Joint Approvals Unit for Periodic Training (JAUPT). Approved training centres deliver courses which a programme of learning of at least seven hours. The seven hours excludes any breaks; only direct training and contact time (time with a trainer) count towards the periodic training requirement. There are no tests or exams involved, but training centres will be required to evaluate each course to ensure that those attending have benefited from the training they have received.

Retraining must take place every 5 years. Drivers have flexibility as to how they take the 35 hours training over this time, providing it occurs in blocks of at least seven hours at one time. So, for example, a driver may complete two days in the first year and the final three days in the fifth year. Similarly they could leave all 35 hours until the fifth year. The retraining must be completed every 5 years until such times as the person no longer wishes to drive category C/C1 (LGV) or D/D1 (PCV) vehicles professionally.

Existing PCV drivers on 10th September 2008 will not have to complete any type of initial qualification. They must have completed all 35 hours of periodic training within 5 years i.e. by 10th September 2013.

Existing LGV drivers on 10th September 2009 do not have to complete any type of initial qualification. They must have completed all 35 hours of periodic training within 5 years i.e. by 10th September 2014.

Periodic training can still be completed if you have been disqualified from driving. A Driver Qualification Card (DQC) will be issued after a driver has completed 35 hours of periodic training.

A DQC is a card that is issued once the theory and practical tests of competence are passed and / or the relevant 'periodic training' is taken. These cards are issued for a 5-year period. A DQC is similar in appearance to the current GB/NI driving licence.

You will only require one DQC which will show all your entitlements. You must carry your DQC with you at all times when you are driving professionally.

HOW TO PASS MODULE 1

These are the subject areas you need to understand to pass Module 1. Most of them you will be aware of to some extent, depending on the amount of experience you already have.

In order to pass the test, remember that Module 1a consists of 100 multiple choice on-screen questions, with a pass mark of 85%. Multiple choice means that you will have to choose from several answers on the screen. One of these will be the correct answer. In general a degree of common sense, together with your existing knowledge and what you study here, will enable you to work out the answer quite easily.

Module 1b consists of 19 video clips containing 20 hazards (HPT - Hazard Perception Test), with a pass mark of 67%. There are numerous sample video clips on the internet, many published by various bodies. It is essential that you familiarise yourself with these clips so that you do not get any surprises when it comes to the test itself. Go onto www.youtube.com or even Google and use the keywords Hazard Perception Test Video. You will get plenty of hits and opportunities to study the sample clips. Bear in mind that these are not the actual clips you will see on the test, for obvious reasons.

Here is a link to get you started.
http://www.youtube.com/watch?v=Zg-INnZ8iXI

You will need to read through all of this but it is not necessary to remember every single fact. The test is multiple choice, which means that the correct answer will be in front of you, together with some incorrect answers as well. You merely need to sort out the correct answer.

Goods Vehicle Weights and Dimensions

WEIGHTS
Maximum Weight

- two-axled rigid vehicles - 18 tonnes
- three-axled rigid vehicles - 26 tonnes
- rigid vehicles with four or more axles - 32 tonnes
- articulated vehicle with three axles - 26 tonnes
- articulated vehicles
    with four axles - 38 tonnes
    with five axles - 40 tonnes
    with six axles - 44 tonnes
- lorry and trailer (ie, drawbar) combinations:
    with four axles - 38 tonnes
    with five axles - 40 tonnes
    with six axles - 44 tonnes
- drive axle - 11.5 tonnes
- tandem-axle bogie - 20 tonnes
- tri-axle bogie - 24 tonnes

Goods Vehicle weights are also dependent on the individual plate for that vehicle.

DIMENSIONS

Maximum Length
- rigid vehicles - 12 metres
- articulated vehicles - 16.5 metres
- drawbar trailers with four or more wheels and drawn by a vehicle over 3,500 kilograms pmw (permissible maximum weight) - 12 metres, ELSE 7 metres
- semi-trailers (used in 16.5-metre articulated combinations kingpin-to-rear end maximum - 12 metres and kingpin-to-front maximum - 2.04 metres
- composite trailer - 14.04 metres
- drawbar combinations - 18.75 metres

Maximum Width
- goods vehicles and trailers - 2.55 metres
- trailer drawn by vehicle up to 3.5 tonnes - 2.3 metres
- refrigerated vehicles and trailers - 2.6 metres

Maximum Height
There is no legal maximum height limit for goods vehicles in Britain, but vehicles must be able to pass under bridges. Motorway bridges and most other unmarked bridges minimum height is 5 metres (16 feet 6 inches).

Secure Loads - Stowage and Safe Loading
There are some good general principles to apply here:

- Make sure your vehicle's load space and the condition of its load platform are suitable for the type and size of your load.
- Make use of load anchorage points.
- Make sure you have enough lashings and that they are in good

condition and strong enough to secure your load.

- Tighten up the lashings or other restraining devices.
- Make sure that the front of the load is abutted against the headboard, or other fixed restraint.
- Use wedges, scotches etc, so that your load cannot move.
- Make sure that loose bulk loads cannot fall or be blown off your vehicle.
- Don't overload your vehicle or its axles.
- Don't load your vehicle too high.
- Don't use rope hooks to restrain heavy loads.
- Don't forget that the size, nature and position of your load will affect the handling of your vehicle.
- Don't forget to check your load before moving off and after you have travelled a few miles, or if you remove or add items to your load during the journey.

Above all, don't take risks.

Principles of Load Safety

When a vehicle changes direction – cornering on roundabouts, overtaking etc., – friction is not enough to stop unsecured cargo from moving. It is wrong to assume that the weight of the load will keep it in position. In fact heavier loads are more likely to move when the vehicle is in motion due to their kinetic energy being greater. Under heavy braking the weight acting in a forward direction can be equal to that acting down on the vehicle. Therefore, a load that is not restrained will not be secure.

The forces acting on the load during braking increase with the rate of deceleration and the weight of the load. So, when the vehicle brakes the load will want to continue to move in its original direction.

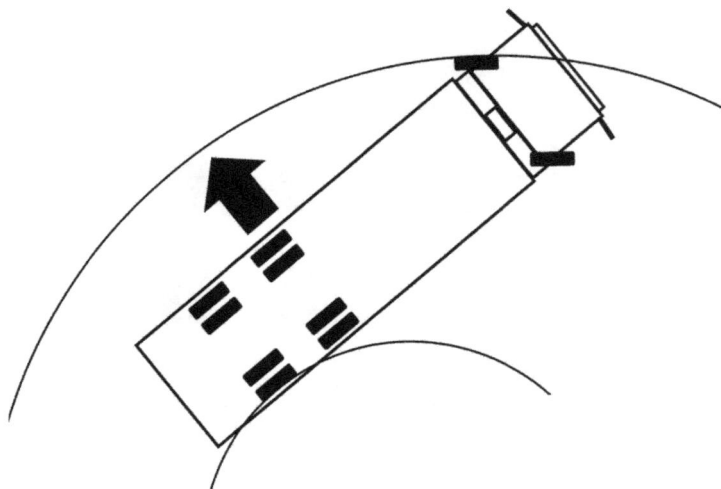

The heavier the load and the harder you brake, the more the load will try to move. Friction alone cannot be relied upon to keep the load in place. When the vehicle is moving, vertical movement caused by bumps will reduce any restraining force due to friction. This can reduce to zero if the load even momentarily leaves the bed of the truck.

It requires much more force to stop a load that has started moving than it does to prevent movement in the first place. This 'battering ram' effect increases rapidly with the increase in distance through which the load moves relative to the vehicle. It is essential therefore that the load is restrained in such a way that movement of the load on the vehicle is prevented. The combined strength of the load restraint system must be sufficient to withstand a force not less than the total weight of the load forward, so as to prevent the load moving under severe braking, and half of the weight of the load backwards and sideways. Vertical movement may occur but this should be overcome if the above conditions are met. This applies to all vehicles no matter what the size, from small vans to the largest goods vehicles. These principles are based on the maximum forces that are likely to be experienced during normal road use. Greater forces may be encountered if the vehicle, for example, is involved in an accident. The principles should therefore be regarded as minimum requirements.

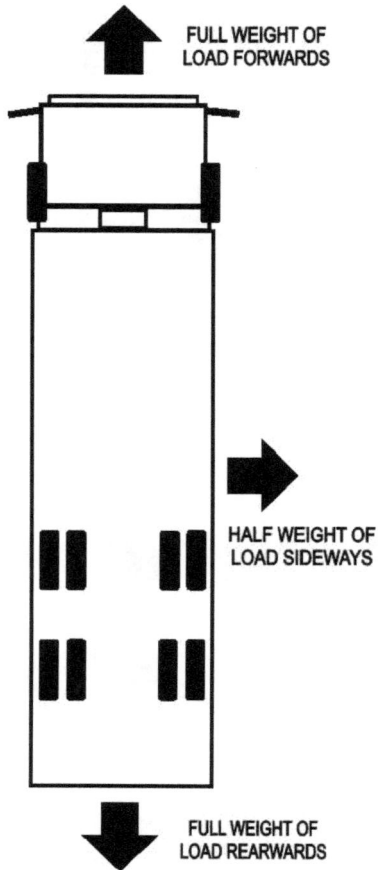

FULL WEIGHT OF LOAD FORWARDS

HALF WEIGHT OF LOAD SIDEWAYS

FULL WEIGHT OF LOAD REARWARDS

The Polluting Effects of Excessive Exhaust Smoke
Diesel engine exhaust emissions have the potential to cause a range of health problems. These emissions (commonly known as 'diesel fumes') are a mixture of gases, vapours, liquid aerosols and substances made up of particles. They contain the products of combustion including:

- carbon (soot)
- nitrogen
- water
- carbon monoxide
- aldehydes
- nitrogen dioxide
- sulphur dioxide
- polycyclic aromatic hydrocarbons

The carbon particle or soot content varies from 60% to 80%, depending on the fuel used and the type of engine. Most of the contaminants are absorbed onto the soot. Petrol engines produce more carbon monoxide but much less soot than diesel engines. The quantity and composition of diesel fumes in your workplace may vary depending on:

- the quality of diesel fuel used
- the type of engine, eg. standard, turbo or injector
- the state of engine tuning
- the fuel pump setting
- the workload demand on the engine
- the engine temperature
- whether the engine has been regularly maintained

Smoke is the product of combustion. Vehicles at your workplace may produce three kinds of smoke, two of which indicate engine problems.

The three types are:

- blue smoke (mainly oil and unburnt fuel) which indicates a poorly serviced and/or tuned engine
- black smoke (soot, oil and unburnt fuel) which indicates a mechanical fault with the engine
- white smoke (water droplets and unburnt fuel) which is produced when the engine is started from cold and disappears when the engine warms up

With older engines, the white smoke produced has a sharp smell which may cause irritation to your upper respiratory system. You should tell your employer if workplace vehicles are producing blue or black smoke so that prompt action can be taken to correct any problem.

Breathing in diesel fumes can affect your health, and exposure to the fumes can cause irritation of your eyes or respiratory tract. These effects are generally short term and should disappear when you are away from the source of exposure. However, prolonged exposure to diesel fumes, in particular to any blue or black smoke, could lead to coughing, chestiness and breathlessness. In the long term, there is some evidence that repeated exposure to diesel fumes over a period of about twenty years may increase the risk of lung cancer. Exposure to petrol engine exhaust emissions does not have the same risk. Skin contact with cold diesel fuel may cause dermatitis. In addition, exhaust smoke can be detrimental to the environment, both humans and animals, as well as having detrimental effects on woodland, grass and growing things generally. Lastly of course there is the problem of increasing damage to the Ozone layer.

Legal Markings on Vehicles

Rear marker boards for the purposes of the lighting regulations fall within Schedule 19. There are 13 Types of marker boards split into 3 sets as follows:

Set 1 - BS AU152 - Type 1 to Type 5
Set 2 - ECE Regulation 70 - Type 6 to Type 9
Set 3 - ECE Regulation 70 Type 10 to Type 13

Motor vehicles with maximum gross weight exceeding 7,500kg first used on or after 1 August 1982 and trailers with maximum gross weight exceeding 3,500kg manufactured on or after 1 August 1982 must be fitted with rear markers. Only vehicles exempt from the prohibition to show any other light but red to the rear by way of rear markings may have them fitted optionally.

Amendments to the lighting regulations mean that goods vehicles first used on or after 1 April 1996, and trailers manufactured on or after 1 October 1995, have to be fitted with new style rear markers with better reflective properties which comply with ECE Regulation 70 rather than British Standard BS AU152. There is no retrospective fitting requirement and 'existing' vehicles can be fitted with markers to the new specification on a voluntary basis.

Specification

The specifications colours are red fluorescent material and yellow reflex reflective material with lettering must be black. Position Rear reflective markers must be fitted to meet the following requirements:

- the markers must be fitted at or near the rear of the vehicle and be securely attached so that no part projects beyond the outermost edge
- the lower edge of the marker must be horizontal and not more than 1,700mm or less than 400mm above the ground, whether the vehicle is laden or unladen
- where the marker consists of one or pairs, these must be fitted as near as practicable to the outermost edge of the vehicle
- rear markers may be fitted to a rearward projecting load instead of to the vehicle if the load would otherwise obscure them. In these circumstances a projecting load marker board need not be fitted
- the markers must remain clearly visible at all times
- although markers are required to be fitted to the 'rear of the vehicle', provided they are clearly visible from the rear they may be fitted as far forward of the rearmost point as may be necessary

First Use/ Manufactured From	Overall Length	Marker Type
A motor vehicle first used on or after 1 April 1996	Not exceeding 13 metres	Type 6, 7, 8 or 9
A motor vehicle first used on or after 1 April 1996	Exceeding 13 metres	Type 10, 11, 12 or 13

A motor vehicle first used before 1 April 1996	Not exceeding 13 metres	Type 1, 2, 3, 6, 7, 8 or 9
A motor vehicle first used before 1 April 1996	Exceeding 13 metres	Type 4, 5, 10, 11, 12 or 13
A trailer manufacturered on or after 1 October 1995 if forming part of a combination with overall length	Not exceeding 11 metres	Type 6, 7, 8 or 9
A trailer manufacturered on or after 1 October 1995 if forming part of a combination with overall length	Exceeding 11 metres but not exceeding 13 metres	Type 6, 7, 8, 9, 10, 11, 12 or 13
A trailer manufacturered on or after 1 October 1995 if forming part of a combination with overall length	exceeding 13 metres	Type 10, 11, 12 or 13
A trailer manufacturered before 1 October 1995 if forming part of a combination with overall length	Not exceeding 11 metres	Type 1, 2, 3, 6, 7, 8 or 9

A trailer manufacturered before 1 October 1995 if forming part of a combination with overall length	Exceeding 11 metres but not exceeding 13 metres	Type 1, 2, 3, 4, 5, 6, 7, 8, 9, 10, 11, 12, or 13
A trailer manufacturered before 1 October 1995 if forming part of a combination with overall length	Exceeding 13 metres	Type 4, 5, 10, 11, 12, or 13

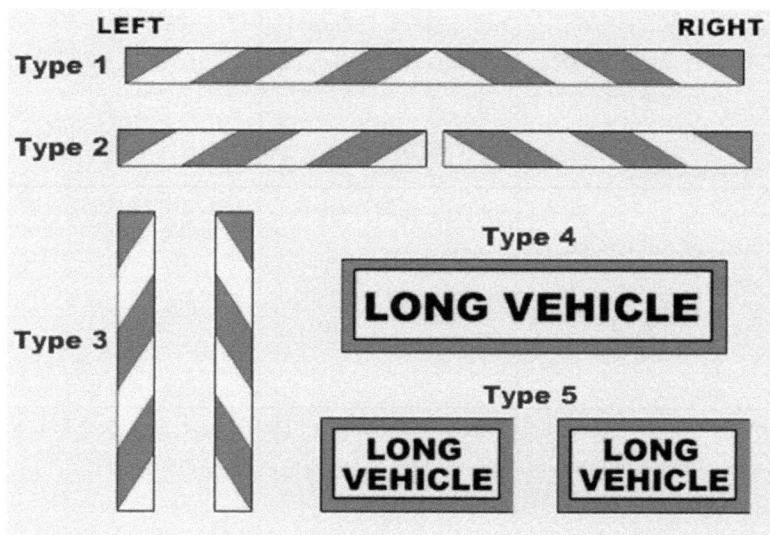

Rear Markings - BS AU152 (Type 1 - 5)

Dimensions for BS AU152

Marking	Length	Width	Other
Type 1	1,400 mm	140 mm	Chevrons must be 45 degrees to the horizontal and should be 140 millimetres width.
Type 2	700 mm	140 mm	Chevrons must be 45 degrees to the horizontal and should be 140 millimetres width and fitted horizontally.
Type 3	700 mm	140 mm	Chevrons must be 45 degrees to the horizontal and should be 140 millimetres width and fitted vertically.
Type 4	1,265 mm	225 mm	The marker plate is banded in red (40 millimetres in depth), with the inner section having black letters (105 millimetres high) on a yellow background.
Type 5	525 mm	250 mm	The marker plate is banded in red (25 millimetres in depth), with the inner section having black letters (70 millimetres high) on a yellow background.

Rear Markings - ECE Regulation 70 - (Type 6 - 9)

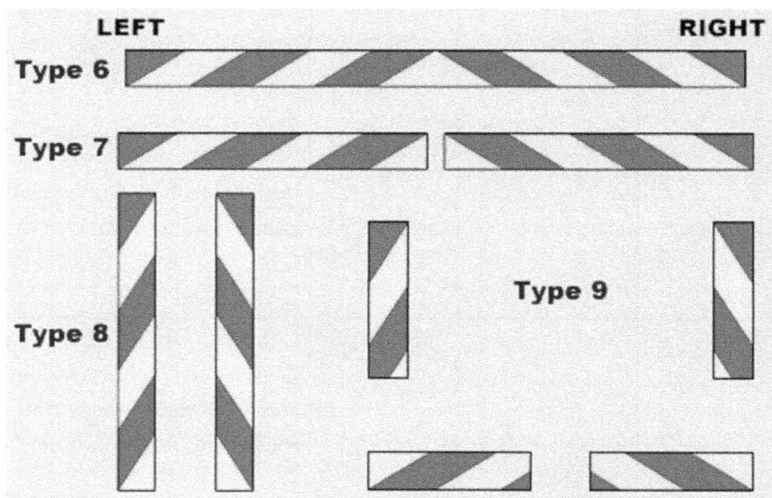

Marking	Length	Width	Dimensions
Type 6	Minimum - 1,130 mm Maximum - 2,300 mm	140 mm	Chevrons must be 45 degrees to the horizontal and should be 140 millimetres width.
Type 7	Minimum - 565 mm Maximum - 1,150 mm	140 mm	Chevrons must be 45 degrees to the horizontal and should be 140 millimetres width.

Type 8	Minimum - 565 mm Maximum - 1,150 mm	140 mm	Chevrons must be 45 degrees to the horizontal and should be 140 millimetres width.
Type 9	283 mm	140 mm	Chevrons must be 45 degrees to the horizontal and should be 140 millimetres width. May be used horizontally or vertically.

Rear Markings - ECE Regulation 70 - (Type 10 - 13)

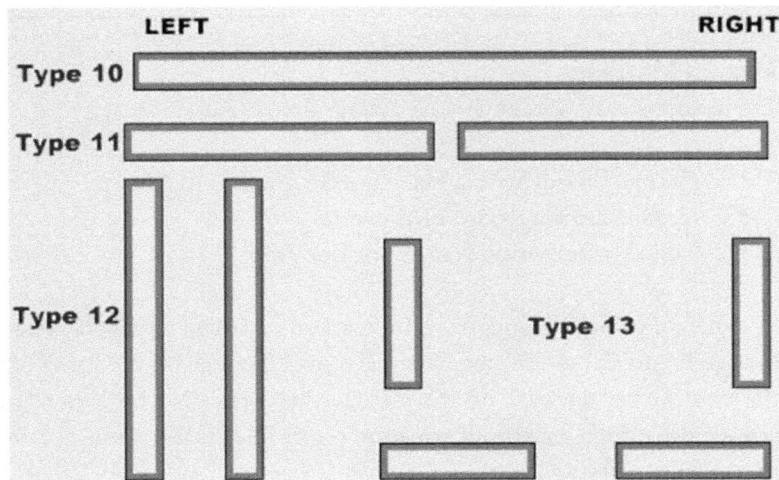

LEFT   RIGHT

Type 10

Type 11

Type 12   Type 13

Marking	Length	Width	Other Dimensions
Type 10	Minimum 1,130 mm - Maximum 2,300 mm	200 mm	Plate should have a red banding (40 millimeters) surrounding a yellow background.
Type 11	Minimum 565 mm - Maximum 1,150 mm	200 mm	Plate should have a red banding (40 millimeters) surrounding a yellow background - fitted horizontally.
Type 12	Minimum 565 mm - Maximum 1,150 mm	200 mm	Plate should have a red banding (40 millimeters) surrounding a yellow background - fitted vertically.
Type 13	283 mm	200 mm	Plate should have a red banding (40 millimeters) surrounding a yellow background. These markers may be fitted horizontally or vertically.

Hazard Markings

There are broadly speaking three types of marking you may see:

- Orange boards with a black border 400mm x 300mm
- Hazard diamonds e.g. Flammable
- Coded information and phone numbers

Where a vehicle is obliged to be marked up it will always have an orange board about the size of a piece of A3 paper on the front of the vehicle. To the rear of the vehicle there will also be either an orange board or a hazard information panel. This is the primary clue to a vehicle carrying dangerous goods.

The hazard diamonds use internationally recognised symbols to show the main hazards of the product. This could be for toxic gas, flammable liquids or even explosives. The coded information is intended for use by those trained to understand it. There are two main components to the coded information. The top number is the Emergency Action Code (EAC) whilst the bottom number is the unique (UN) number for the produce being carried. In addition there may be a specialist advice phone number. This enables the Hazardous Materials (HazMat) advisor to gain advice from an expert with regards to how to tackle an incident.

What is an EAC?
In the UK the Emergency Action Code is a two or three digit code made up of one number and one or two letters. If there are two letters it will have an 'E' at the end of it. If that is the case then the load poses a public safety hazard. The emergency services will manage the incident but if you are first on the scene then all non-essential personnel should be moved to a minimum of 250 metres from the vehicle. Internationally the convention is different and the emergency action code is made up of only numbers. These tell you about the hazards of the load but do not tell you if the product is a public safety hazard for example. If in any doubt take advice from a trained hazmat advisor.

What is the UN Number?
The UN number for a particular produce remains constant across the world. This is a 4-digit number which is unique to that product. For example, UN1203 is petrol and UN1001 is acetylene. The linked document is very useful as it provides information to the fire service on how to fight fires and what protective equipment to use. To the untrained eye it is simple a list of codes but it does allow you to look up what a vehicle is carrying using only the UN number. It also contains examples of the hazard diamonds and an interpretation guide to the various coding.

Vehicle Braking Systems
Types of Brake and How they Work

Road Vehicles (Construction and Use) Regulations 1986 states that where a trailer required to be fitted with brakes is drawn by a motor vehicle the driver shall be in a position to operate the brakes to the motor vehicle and the trailer unless :-

• the trailer is fitted with overrun brakes, or the trailer is a broken down vehicle being drawn in such a manner that it cannot be steered by it's own steering. (If the vehicle is not broken down or otherwise exempt then it cannot, for instance, be towed front suspended for delivery without some form of automatic braking system fitted).

Automatic Slack Adjuster Unbraked Trailers
Regulation 87 Road Vehicles (Construction and Use) Regulations 1986 concerns unbraked trailers where it is overloaded (its laden weight exceeds its maximum gross weight), or where the weight of the trailer plus its load exceeds half the kerbside weight of the drawing vehicle.

Therefore, brakes are required on a small trailer (unless the trailer falls within another exemption or is an agricultural trailer) if it is overladen, or if the kerbside weight of the drawing vehicle is less than twice the total actual weight of the trailer; e.g. a 500 kg gross unbraked trailer must be towed by a motor vehicle with a kerbside weight of a least 1000 kg. The type of braking system required to be fitted to a vehicle depends on its type and age. EC braking requirements (regulation 15) would therefore apply in the main, to vehicles first used on or after 1st April 1983. Construction and Use requirements (regulation 16) apply to all other vehicles except those listed within the regulations as being exempt.

No person shall use, or cause or permit to be used, on a road an unbraked wheeled trailer if:

- its laden weight exceeds its maximum gross weight or
- it is drawn by a vehicle of which the kerbside weight is less than twice the sum of the unladen weight of the trailer and the weight of any load which the trailer is carrying

This regulation does not apply to an agricultural trailer.

Introduction to ABS
The abbreviation ABS stands for anti-lock braking system. The purpose of this system is to prevent the wheels from locking when the brakes are applied when the brake force generated exceeds that which can be transmitted to the road via the tyre.

A great benefit with the ABS system is that it provides a maximum exploitation of the available road surface friction when the brakes are applied. Consequently the braking distance is considerably shorter and the vehicle is much easier to control under emergency braking.

If the vehicle is pulling a trailer the most efficient conditions are when both the tractor and trailer are equipped with non-locking brakes.

The ABS system is governed by a control unit (micro-computer) which senses the wheel speeds with the aid of a sensor and a pole wheel or exciter ring fitted to the brake drum or disc. The signals from the sensor are processed by the control unit, which, via solenoid valves, governs the braking pressure of the individual wheel brake actuators. Where axles form a bogie, it may only have sensors fitted to one of the axles forming the bogie. The ABS system includes a number of control functions that test the individual electrical circuits to ensure that they are functioning correctly. Should a fault occur the driver is informed by a warning lamp on his instrument panel or, if a trailer is being drawn, via a lamp visible to the driver on the front of the trailer.

Categories of ABS Towing Vehicles

Category 1

The ABS will operate on at least one front axle and on one rear axle and have the ability to utilise the higher adhesion when braking on a split friction surface. This will require one of the axles, usually the rear axle, to have independent control. A typical system would have four sensors and four modulators but could effectively have four sensors and two or three modulators. In the latter case the front axle could use one modulator with a "Select Low" control philosophy where modulation action is taken on the first wheel to lock. This system will protect the towing vehicle from brake induced jack-knifing and enable the driver to steer during braking by preventing the directly controlled wheels from locking.

Category 2

The ABS will operate on at least one front axle and on one rear axle. The system will have a minimum of four sensors and two modulators (one for each axle). The system will generally operate on a "select Low" control philosophy where modulation action will be taken on the first wheel to lock. This system will protect the towing vehicle from brake induced jack-knifing and enable the driver to steer during braking by preventing the directly controlled wheels from locking.

Category 3

The ABS operates only on the rear (drive) axle. The system will have two sensors and one modulator and generally a "select Low" control philosophy where modulation action will be taken on the first wheel to lock. This system will protect the towing vehicle from brake induced jack-knifing by preventing the directly controlled wheels from locking.

TRAILERS

Category A

A trailer with a Category A ABS will meet the split friction deceleration requirements. Only trailers approved under the carriage of dangerous goods regulations (ADR) must have a Category A system. The minimum requirement for a Category A semi-trailer would be for two sensors and two modulators. Each modulator would control the wheels on one side of the trailer. The minimum requirement for a Category A full drawbar trailer (a turntable type) is four sensors and three modulators. In this case the rear axle would be independently controlled.

Category B

A trailer with a Category B ABS does not need to meet the split friction deceleration requirements. The minimum requirement for either a semi-trailer or a centre axle drawbar trailer is two sensors and one modulator. On a full drawbar (turntable type) the minimum requirement would be two sensors and two modulators, although four sensors and three modulators is the industry practice.

Maintenance and Inspection of Vehicle brakes

See vehicle daily walkaround in appendix 1

VEHICLE BRAKING AND SPEED CONTROLS

Basics of Heavy Vehicle Brakes

Drivers should understand the basics of the braking system on heavy vehicles and, where appropriate, the connections between vehicles and trailers. Heavy vehicle braking systems have progressed over the years from simple mechanically operated contraptions, through hydraulic and vacuum systems, to the highly efficient and technologically sophisticated air-brake systems that we have today. These use compressed air produced from an engine-mounted compressor to provide the operating force.

Additionally, most modern vehicles are fitted with anti-lock braking systems (ABS), which effectively prevent wheel locking under heavy braking, and retarders (or endurance brakes), which add to the braking effect by slowing the rotation of the transmission system with electro-magnetic devices or by exhaust gases diverted into an exhauster linked into the braking system. Retarders are best suited to slowing vehicles on long downhill runs where the main brakes may become overheated and begin to fade.

Heavy vehicles usually have three separate braking systems, comprising:

- service brakes
- secondary brakes
- parking brakes (on the vehicle and also on the trailer or semi-trailer)

The service brake is the principal braking system used and is operated via the foot pedal on the wheel brakes (usually drum-type brakes, but increasingly these days, disc brakes). This brake is used to control the speed of the vehicle and to stop it safely when required.

The secondary brake is usually combined with either the foot brake or the parking brake control.

The parking brake is usually a hand control mounted on the steering column or the dashboard — it may also be the secondary braking system. Normally, the parking brake is used only when the vehicle is stationary to ensure it cannot move when the driver leaves the driving cab. It is an offence to leave a vehicle unattended without setting the parking brake.

Trailer Connections
It is vital to understand the rules that apply to connecting and disconnecting brake lines on either an articulated vehicle or a rigid vehicle and drawbar trailer combination.

Drivers are required to demonstrate this procedure during the practical driving test.

Two different brake configurations may be encountered,either a three-airline system or a two-airline system.

A three-line system comprises the emergency line (coloured red), the auxiliary line (coloured blue) and the service line (coloured yellow) whereas a two-line system has only emergency and service airlines.

Connecting two-line vehicles and two-line trailers is not difficult because they appear clearly compatible, as are three-line vehicles and three-line trailers. However, a two-line tractive unit can be connected to a three-line trailer with the trailer auxiliary line being left unconnected. But caution is needed when connecting a three-line tractive unit to a two-line trailer. In this case it is important to follow the vehicle manufacturer's advice as to what to do with the third (blue) line. Failure to follow such instructions could result in a dangerous situation with the combination brakes not operating effectively.

Airlines

The function of the airline is to carry compressed air from the tractive unit to the semi-trailer for the purpose of braking nylon air-coils, commonly known as susies, are fitted to most tractive units. They overcome the disadvantages normally associated with the old rubber hose-type airlines. All airline coils are internationally colour coded (red, blue and yellow — see above) and are capable of extending to such a length that they remain fully operational even when the articulated vehicle is in a complete jack-knife position.

Safe procedure for Stowing Airlines

When disconnecting airlines, for the purposes of uncoupling the trailer, it is sensible to start with the one nearest and stow them away, one at a time. When connecting airlines, follow the opposite procedure, starting with the one furthest away. This practice reduces the risk of accidentally tripping over the coils, and helps to keep them from becoming tangled.

Brake Line Adaptors

Most articulated vehicles in the United Kingdom are equipped with standard male/female adaptors, which reduce the risk of wrong connection. Some, however, use 'palm-couplings', which are all alike, and great care must be exercised to ensure that incorrect connections are not made, which can render the trailer brakes inoperative. The colour coding is the reliable key.

Non-return Valves and Air Taps

Modern braking systems have non-return valves located within the air-brake system allowing the air pressure to be immediately shut off, or automatically as the airlines are disconnected or reconnected. On older braking systems manual air taps are fitted, which the driver must operate himself when connecting and disconnecting the brakes. Where such taps are fitted into the airlines, it is important that they are turned off before disconnecting the airlines. If this is not done, it will result in an immediate air loss from the red emergency line and will render the yellow service line and the blue auxiliary line ineffective when the brakes are applied. It is equally important that the air taps are turned on again after airlines have been connected. If this is not done, the trailer brakes will be totally inoperable.

ANTI-LOCK (ABS) BRAKES

ABS is the registered trademark of German firm Bosch and stands for Anti-Blockiersystem (ie, anti-lock braking system). Many modern heavy vehicles, and cars too, are equipped with anti-lock braking systems — some are compulsorily fitted by law. These systems use electrically powered speed sensors (with multi-pin connectors and cables carrying the electrical supply to the trailer brakes) to anticipate when a wheel is about to lock up under braking (e.g. especially on wet or slippery surfaces). Just before lock-up happens the system releases the brake and then reapplies it rapidly many times in quick succession. This provides virtually continuous braking to the wheel without the dangers of skidding that would result if the wheel locked. Preventing the wheels from locking also means that the driver is still able to steer the vehicle during braking.

Note:
ABS fitment is legally required for goods vehicles over 16 tonnes gross weight first used since April 1992, for goods vehicles over 3.5 tonnes gross weight first registered from April 2002 and for goods-

carrying trailers over 3.5 tonnes gross weight first used since this date.

Checking the ABS

The driver should ensure that the ABS on his vehicle/trailer is functioning correctly before setting out on a journey. Driving with a defective ABS is illegal. Satisfactory operation of the ABS can be checked via the warning instrument/light on the vehicle dashboard with a separate warning instrument/light signal for the trailer mounted either on the vehicle dashboard or, in some cases, on the trailer headboard. Warning light signals operate differently between manufacturers, but in all cases the signal should be displayed when the ignition is switched on and should go out no later than when the vehicle has reached a road speed of about 10 kph (6 mph).

Technique for Driving with ABS

ABS is only an aid to the driver; it does not replace good driving techniques and is not provided to allow last-minute braking as a regular practice. The driver should still anticipate what is happening on the road ahead and should assess traffic flow and road surface conditions to allow plenty of time for normal braking. However, when it is necessary to exert greater pressure on the brakes for a quick stop, the driver will feel the cadence (hammering) effect through the brake pedal as the system pumps the brakes on and off very rapidly. He should ignore this and continue to press the pedal in the normal way, allowing the ABS to work effectively.

ENDURANCE BRAKES — RETARDERS

Endurance brakes are commonly referred to as 'retarders'. These are braking systems that enable vehicle speed to be controlled without using the normal wheel brakes. They are especially useful when descending long gradients, saving wear on the service brakes as well as avoiding the risk of reduced braking performance due to brake fade — caused by overheating of the drums and linings. The use of a retarder allows the service brakes to remain cool ready for when they are needed.

Use of Brakes and Retarders

Skilled drivers can combine the use of the footbrake and retarder on the vehicle to provide smooth driving, particularly essential when driving a coach load of passengers or a load of livestock, but equally commendable when driving goods vehicles. Significantly too, such use can save considerably on the costs of brake and tyre wear and in fuel consumption.

The skill is that of being aware of the road and traffic conditions ahead and adjusting the vehicle speed accordingly by judicious use of the retarder in good time, not leaving it until the last minute when approaching an obstacle, a bend in the road or a traffic sign, which may result in the need for heavy braking. Looking and being aware of what is ahead is the sign of a skilful LGV driver.

LOW-PRESSURE WARNINGS

Air-brake systems are fitted with warning devices (lights and buzzers) that are activated when air pressure in the system falls below a predetermined level. No attempt should be made to move a vehicle when the brake pressure warning system is operating. Similarly, if the warning activates while the vehicle is moving, it should be brought to a standstill quickly and safely, and not be moved again until the defect is rectified. Driving with a warning device operating is very dangerous and is an offence.

Brake Failure — What to Do

Only in the rarest of circumstances do modern heavy vehicle air-braking systems fail leaving the vehicle totally uncontrollable. It is to ensure against this that vehicles are equipped with three types of brakes:

- service brakes providing a minimum of 50% braking efficiency
- secondary brakes providing a minimum of 25% braking efficiency
- a parking brake

Should one part of the system fail (ie through loss of air pressure), besides being given an audible or visual warning in the cab, the driver would have an adequate reserve of air pressure in the secondary system to enable him to stop the vehicle safely.

DRIVER CHECKS

Drivers must check that the braking system of their vehicle is working satisfactorily before driving on the road, irrespective of how short the journey. Before each journey they should make sure that all warning systems are working correctly and should note whether brake pressure warning signals activate automatically when the ignition is turned on (as for the ABS), or whether a switch on the dashboard has to be operated to check the system.

Draining the Air Tanks

Where necessary the driver should also use the manual drain valves on the air tanks (reservoirs) to release any moisture that has been drawn into the system and that may freeze on frosty mornings forming ice in valves and pipework. This may result in loss of air pressure or even system failure. Some air systems have automatic drain valves to remove moisture, making this task unnecessary.

The Hand Brake

When uncoupling a trailer, and before disconnecting any of the brake lines, the driver must ensure that the trailer parking brake has been correctly applied. Without this safety step being carried out, the trailer could move when the airlines are disconnected.

SPEED LIMITERS

The law requires speed limiters to be fitted to certain heavy goods vehicles to prevent over-speeding and thereby help to reduce road accidents. Also, driving at a reduced speed (i.e. within the legal limits set for speed limiters) means considerable benefit will accrue to operators in terms of fuel economy. This saving as much as 150 million litres annually according to the UK government, and helping the environment by an annual reduction of some 0.5 million tonnes of carbon monoxide from exhaust emissions pumped into the atmosphere.

UK regulations limit all new goods vehicles over 7.5 tonnes maximum gross weight (with certain special exceptions) to a maximum speed of 60 mph (96 kph). The speed limiter must be maintained in good working order, but where a vehicle is driven with a defective limiter, it is a defence to show that the defect occurred during that journey or that at the time it was being driven to a place for the limiter to be repaired.

EU Requirements

EU regulations require over-12-tonne goods vehicles to have their speed limiter set to a maximum speed of not more than 85 kph 3mph), allowing a stabilised speed of not more than 90 kph (56 mph). The only other exemptions are where a speed limiter has failed on a journey and the journey is being completed or when the vehicle is being taken to a place for the speed limiter to be repaired or replaced.

Speed Limiter Plates

Vehicles covered by the above-mentioned regulations must be

fitted with a speed limiter plate fitted in a conspicuous and readily accessible position in the vehicle cab.

Preventive Maintenance for Vehicle Air Brakes

The air brakes on tractor-trailers need regular maintenance. The air brakes on big rigs can overheat and malfunction when for example driving a fully loaded 80,000 tractor and fully loaded trailer safely down a steep mountain road. Preventive maintenance plays a key role in making sure air brakes function properly and pass Department of Transport safety inspections.

Air Lines

Air lines must be in good shape to work properly.

Air lines must not be cracked, frayed or otherwise damaged. To prevent chafing, make sure they are not rubbing against other parts of the vehicle. Draining the air tank daily keeps moisture from building up in the system. Moisture could make it harder to stop in cold weather.

Brake Pads

Brake pads should wear evenly. Inspect brake pads for cracks or other damage. Make sure there is no oil or grease from leaking hub seals or axle seals. The brake pads should be at least a quarter-inch thick.

Adjusters

If maintained properly, adjusters ensure that each brake receives equal pressure. Improper adjustment may cause pads to wear unevenly and make it harder to stop.

Air Pressure

Loss of air pressure means your truck will not move. Check the air pressure in the air tank on a regular basis. Air brakes require between 100 and 140 pounds per square inch to function properly. If the pressure dips to about 60 psi, warning lights or buzzers should come on in the cabin.The risks and Adverse Effects of Tailgating

Many rear-end collisions are caused by tailgating. It is estimated that the average driver brakes 50,000 times a year to avoid a rear-end collision. When drivers tailgate they significantly reduce their stopping distance, the distance needed to come to a complete and safe stop. What many drivers do not realise is that stopping distance is directly proportional to the size and weight of the vehicle. For example, the stopping distance is much longer for a heavy truck than it is for a passenger vehicle, such as a car. In fact, it takes about twice the distance to stop a heavy truck than it does a car. Other critical driving elements drivers sacrifice when tailgating are perception and reaction times. These are two separate intervals of time.

Perception is the time needed to see and process a roadway hazard, while reaction time is the time needed for a driver's body to physically react to their brain's perception. When a driver tailgates they significantly reduce both. It can take alert drivers approximately two seconds to see a roadway hazard and react to it. The more space a driver allows between their vehicle and the vehicle in front of them, the more time they have to see a hazard and react safely.

A driver's best defence against becoming involved in a rear-end collision is to create a "safety cushion" by keeping at least two seconds between them and the vehicle in front of them. This allows time for the driver to perceive and react to a roadway hazard, ultimately, avoiding an accident. For added protection when driving in poor conditions, such as driving at night, in bad weather, in heavy traffic and through roadway construction, drivers should upgrade to four seconds.

The Effects of Freezing Weather Conditions on Vehicle Braking Systems

Cold weather by itself does not affect braking much, provided the brake system is in good working order. Most brake pads do not grab efficiently until they get hot, ceramic pads especially, but the brakes get hot within seconds of application and remain plenty warm enough until the vehicle is parked. There is always light contact between the pads and rotors.

However, moisture in the brake system can freeze and prevent application or cause the brakes to hang up and stay applied. Additionally, moisture in a brake system that is hot can boil and cause the brakes to fade badly once the vehicle has been driven a few miles. Brake fluid is hygroscopic, meaning it absorbs moisture, so the fluid should be flushed at the manufacturer's recommended interval to prevent these problems.

On a snowy or wet day, when the brakes are continually getting wet, the temperature of the rotors/drums is 20-30% higher than it is on a dry day. This is due to the water acting as a lubricant on the brake parts and the increased hydraulic force it takes to achieve enough friction to stop the vehicle. Drastic temperature fluctuations cause rotors to warp and will make the brake pedal pulsate on application. Be aware of this when driving in poor conditions. It is sensible to stop more gently because of slippery road conditions and it will also prolong brake life and help to prevent vibrations while braking.

How Power Steering Systems Work

Most power steering systems work by using a hydraulic system to turn the vehicle's wheels. The hydraulic pressure is usually provided by a gerotor or rotary vane pump driven by the vehicle's engine. A double-acting hydraulic cylinder applies a force to the steering gear, which in turn applies a torque to the steering axis of the road wheels. The flow to the cylinder is controlled by valves operated by the steering wheel; the more torque the driver applies to the steering wheel and the shaft it is attached to, the more fluid the valves allow through to the cylinder, and so the more force is applied to steer the wheels in the appropriate direction.

One design for measuring the torque applied to the steering wheel is to fix a torsion bar to the end of the steering shaft. As the steering wheel rotates, so does the attached steering shaft, and so does the top end of the attached torsion bar. Since the torsion bar is relatively thin and flexible and the bottom end is not completely free to rotate, the bar will soak up some of the torque; the bottom end will not rotate as far as the top end. The difference in rotation between the top and bottom ends of the torsion bar can be used to control the valve that allows fluid to flow to the cylinder which provides steering assistance; the greater the "twist" of the torsion bar, the more steering assistance will be provided.

Since the pumps employed are of the positive displacement type, the flow rate they deliver is directly proportional to the speed of the engine. This means that at high engine speeds the steering would naturally operate faster than at low engine speeds. Because this would be undesirable, a restricting orifice and flow control valve are used to direct some of the pump's output back to the hydraulic reservoir at high engine speeds. A pressure relief valve is also used to prevent a dangerous build-up of pressure when the hydraulic cylinder's piston reaches the end of the cylinder.

Some modern implementations also include an electronic pressure relief valve which can reduce the hydraulic pressure in the power steering lines as the vehicle's speed increases (this is known as variable assist power steering).

The Law on Speed Limiters

From 1 January 2007 additional vehicles fell into the scope under the speed limiter legislation introduced in January 2005. The changes affected all goods vehicles over 3.5 tonnes maximum gross weight and all passenger vehicles with 8 or more passenger seats, irrespective of weight. The relevant date for fitting speed limiters varies depending on the gross design weight of the vehicle, engine type (such as Euro III), international or national usage and the date of first registration.

Specifically affected from January 2007 are goods vehicles between 3.5 and 7.5 tonnes and passenger vehicles with more than 8 seats, irrespective of weight, which were first registered between 1 October 2001 and 31 December 2004, have Euro III engines approved to Directive 88/77/EEC and are used on national operations in this country.

In addition, goods vehicles first registered between 1 October 2001 and 31 December 2004 with a maximum gross weight between 7.5 tonnes and 12 tonnes, have to have their existing speed limitation devices recalibrated from 60mph to 56mph.

If a vehicle has, or is required to have, a speed limiter fitted and working, then it is not permitted to use the outside lane of a three or more lane motorway. If the vehicle is required to have a speed limiter fitted but it is not working, it will be illegal to use it on the public highway under the Road Vehicles (Construction and Use) Regulations 1986

Requirements
The New Speed Limiter Regulations apply to:

- passenger vehicles over 8 seats but not over 7500 kg Design Gross Vehicle Weight (DGVW)
- goods vehicles over 3500 kg but not over 7500 kg DGVW

The regulations apply depending on vehicle age as follows:

- Vehicles first used prior to 1 October 2001 - No requirement.

- Vehicles first used on or after 1 October 2001 up to and including 31 December 2004 - For British domestic use only will require a speed limiter set such that the vehicle speed cannot exceed
- 100 kph (passenger vehicles) (62.14 mph) or
- 90 kph (goods vehicles) (56 mph)

The above were required to be fitted by 1 January 2007 if they had a Euro 3 engine with emissions approval under directive 88/77/EC. There are two categories of vehicles that are currently required to have speed limiters fitted by UK domestic regulations, which will need to have the set speed of the systems changed.

These vehicles are:

1. Goods vehicles (with a gross design weight over 7.5t but not exceeding 12.0t, first registered between 1 October 2001 and 31 October 2004) which will need to have the speed limiters reset so the current maximum set speed of 60 mph will be replaced by a reduced setting that will ensure the stabilised speed cannot exceed 90kph.
2. Passenger vehicles (with more than 8 passenger seats and a design weight over 7.5t and not exceeding 10.0t) which will need to have the speed limiters reset so the current set speed of 100kph will need to be reduced to a setting that will ensure that the maximum stabilised speed will not exceeding 100kph.

There are also separate provisions that apply to passenger vehicles with over 8 passenger seats and a design weight over 10.0t gross that are already fitted with a speed limiter set at 100kph. These vehicles will not be required to have the speed limiters reset and will be able to continue with systems set at 100kph.

There are retro-fit requirements that apply to goods (over 3.5t GDW) and passenger vehicles (over 8 passenger seats - irrespective of weight) that were first registered between 1 October 2001 and 31 December 2004 (inclusive).

Vehicles caught by these requirements needed to be fitted with speed limiters with effect from 1 January 2006, unless the vehicle was used solely within the UK, in which case the requirement came into effect on 1 January 2007.

Drivers' Hours Rules and Rest Period Requirements

You must take a daily rest period within twenty four hours of the previous daily or weekly rest period. A regular daily rest period is defined as a rest of at least eleven hours.

According to the European Union (EU) drivers' hours rules, a 'rest' is an uninterrupted period where you may do what you like. Time that is spent working for yourself or others, no matter what the occupation, cannot be counted as rest. Time that you spend learning or doing something under obligation is also not counted as rest.

You also have the option to split a regular daily rest period into two periods. The first period must be at least three hours of continuous rest and taken at any time during the day. The second must be at least nine hours of continuous rest, giving a total minimum rest of twelve hours. For example, a 24-hour period can be broken down into:

- eight hours of driving, other work and breaks
- three hours of rest
- four hours of driving, other work and breaks
- a nine hour rest period

You may reduce your daily rest period to no fewer than nine continuous hours, with no need to make up for this. However, you can do this no more than three times between any two weekly rest periods. If your daily rest is less than eleven hours but at least nine hours, it is called a reduced daily rest period.

You can take your daily rest in a vehicle, if it has suitable sleeping facilities and is stationary. If you begin work at 06.00 on day one, then by 06.00 on day two you must complete one of the following:

- a regular daily rest period of at least eleven hours
- a split daily rest period of at least twelve hours
- a reduced daily rest period of at least nine hours - if you are entitled

Weekly Rest Periods

You must take a weekly rest period within six days of the end of the last weekly rest period. However, from 4 June 2010, coach drivers on single international journeys are able to postpone their weekly rest period until the end of the twelfth day (this rule cannot be applied to domestic trips). These drivers must also take a regular forty-five hour rest prior to the journey beginning, in addition to at least one regular and one reduced weekly rest period back to back on the journey's completion, which amounts to a minimum rest period of at least sixty nine hours.

A weekly rest period is a period during which you may freely dispose of your time, and can be either a 'regular weekly rest period' or a 'reduced weekly rest period'.

A regular weekly rest period is a period of at least forty-five consecutive hours. A reduced weekly rest period must be a minimum of twenty-four consecutive hours. If you take a reduced rest, then you must compensate for the reduction with an equal period of rest. This should be taken in one block by the end of the third week following the week in which the reduction is taken. The compensating rest must be attached to a period of rest of at least nine hours – i.e. either a weekly or daily rest period.

Requirements on Record Keeping

Maintaining records for working time should be undertaken in the same manner in which vehicle or staff records are kept, in a logical and easy to access manner. However, if you decide to maintain records electronically, we believe these should be maintained as follows:

All electronic records should be backed up to a CD rom upon each weeks completion.

Each weeks data should be printed off and clipped to all timesheets and/or clocking in/out data sheets used in the calculations.

Keep the 'hard copy' data in A4 folders marked with what it applies to, (e.g. WTD Data) from date to date. This is particularly useful if you are collating data for more than one depot

Calculating WTD Data

It isn't necessary for you to worry about undertaking your own WTD calculations, you can use the services of an outside source, such as the FTA, RHA, a tachograph analysis company or a transport consultant to do it for you. However, if you have the resources or operate a small operation, it will inevitably be cheaper to do this yourself.

Calculating working time is fairly straightforward. However, if you decide to maintain your records using a spreadsheet, it must be remembered that spreadsheets calculate in decimal places as a percentage of 100, and whereas an hour is made up of 60 minutes, recording hours and minutes on a spreadsheet is not the same as inputting hours with the minutes re-calculated as a percentage.

The Law on Tachographs

An approved tachograph is the required instrument by which the activities of drivers subject to the EU or AETR drivers' hours rules, and the vehicle's speed, distance and time are recorded. There are two main types of tachograph - analogue and digital. The only exception is when driving a vehicle engaged in the collecting of sea coal. In this one case you are subject to the EU rules on drivers' hours but do not need a tachograph.

The resulting record is to be used to monitor compliance with rules on drivers' hours. The rules on using the tachograph are contained in Regulation (EC) 3821/85 (as amended), and these depend on whether the vehicle is fitted with an analogue or digital tachograph. These rules must be observed by both drivers and operators of vehicles that fall within the scope of Regulation (EC) 561/2006 or the AETR rules. There is an extensive book published by the Department for Transport on current tachograph legislation that you can download for free from:

http://www.dft.gov.uk/pgr/freight/road/workingtime/drivershoursgoods.pdf

The Effects of Tiredness on Drivers
Around 20% of the accidents that occur on motorways happen as a direct result of motorists falling asleep at the wheel. A survey in Ireland revealed that almost two in every five motorists said they had suffered from driver fatigue over the last year, and one in eight actually admitted to nodding off at the wheel of their vehicle at least once.

Some research into tired driving habits shows that too little sleep can be as detrimental to a driver's responses as drinking alcohol.

Crashes on motorways, thought to be caused by tired drivers, are typically identified by drivers running off the road or smashing into the back of another vehicle. Of course, the collisions tend to be high-speed, because the driver is not alert enough to brake before the crash occurs.

What can you do to reduce the risk?

- Make sure you are getting enough sleep, and do not even think about setting off on a long journey without getting a good night's sleep first.
- Plan a break into your journey - fifteen minutes for every two hours driving.
- Remember that the risks of tiredness increase if you have to get up unusually early to begin your trip. If you feel sleepy or drowsy find a safe place to stop and sleep as soon as you can. (Not the hard shoulder!)
- Drinking a few cups of coffee, or high caffeine drink and allowing time for the caffeine to become effective (twenty - thirty minutes) can be a good method of staying awake. Unlike opening the window or turning up the radio - they are likely to have little, if any effect on a sleepy driver.

Remember that if you are tired, alcohol will affect your body far more than usual, to the point where one drink when tired can have a similar effect to four or five drinks when you are at normal levels of alertness. Do not rely on a 'mind over matter' technique to stay awake. You are more likely to lull yourself off to sleep than you are to keep yourself awake. You have no control when you are too tired to stay awake.

Driver Responsibility for the Security of Vehicle and Load
As a driver your employer and customers will expect you to look after your vehicle and load responsibly and carefully. Here are some steps you should always remember to take.

- The cab of the vehicles must be locked at all times whenever the vehicle is left unattended.
- Drivers are required to exercise maximum care to prevent

thefts.

- Vehicles fitted with alarms/immobilisers must never be left unattended without the security system being fully operational.
- Any expensive / attractive items should be locked away or removed from the vehicle.
- Particular attention should be paid to portable satellite navigation systems.

At all times, drivers should be responsible for the care, security and safety of their vehicle's load and must exercise the maximum care to prevent loss, damage or theft.

Any vehicle over three metres in height must display a notice of the vehicle height in a prominent position in the vehicle cab. The height must be displayed in feet and inches. Alternatively, documents must be carried detailing the route to be taken, with no obstacles. There is a limit of 4.2 metres in height of any load carried on an LGV. There is a particular need for drivers to take care when their vehicles are pulling high loads or trailers especially when negotiating low bridges.

The safest rule is always; if in doubt – get out and have a look – Don't take a chance.

REMEMBER:
Bridges over 16.6 feet do not have to show their height.

Drivers are reminded of the need to take particular care with the documentation for any load and always to ensure that the correct procedures and associated paperwork, are completed and that the condition of loads is inspected where practical and any discrepancies in either quantity or condition are noted and photographed if possible.

Stability of High and Long Vehicles

Stability of high sided and long vehicles will be affected by a range of factors, especially high winds and certain types of roads, e.g.long downhill stretches especially with bends. It is extremely important to allow for these factors as well as the following that affect the various types of load that may be carried.

- Know the weight limits for your vehicle including axle weights.

The total load restraint system will generally consist of a combination of lashings secured to anchorage points attached to the vehicle chassis, which includes bars etc, which are securely attached to the vehicle, and friction between the load and the vehicle platform.

- Always check the weight of the load to be carried.
- Remember that the size, type and weight of the load will affect the handling of the vehicle.
- Check the load before moving off and whenever items are added or removed.
- Remember that loads can settle and shift during a journey causing lashings to slacken.
- Check the load at regular intervals and after heavy braking or sudden changes in direction.
- Don't overload the vehicle or axles.
- Don't load the vehicle too high
- Don't reduce the on the steered axle by positioning the load too far back.
- Don't move the vehicle with any part of the load not restrained.
- Don't climb onto the vehicle or its load unless it is essential and there is a safe means of access.

When a vehicle changes direction — cornering on roundabouts, overtaking etc, take extra care. Under heavy braking, the weight acting in a forward direction can be equal to that acting down the vehicle. Therefore, a load that is not restrained will not be secure. The forces acting on the load during braking increase with the rate of deceleration and the weight of the load. The weight of heavy loads of small dimensions should be distributed across the vehicle platform by the use of load spreading devices, (e.g. pallets, large wooden boards etc.)

How to Reduce the Risk of Road Accidents

- Be aware of your surroundings. Most traffic accidents can be avoided if the driver pays attention to surroundings such as traffic signs and other drivers. You should always pay attention to traffic signs and signals, because if you don't you could face more than just a wreck, you could face hefty penalties, loss of employment, insurance rate increase and even a fatal accident. Make sure you notice and obey all traffic signs and pay attention to your fellow motorists.

- Travel at a safe speed. Speed limit signs are the most often ignored traffic signs in Europe. Travelling at a safe speed can save you a speeding ticket. Speed kills. It is recommended that you obey speed limit signs primarily to save your life and the life of drivers around you.

- Travel safely during adverse weather conditions. During snow and rain especially, the roads are slicker than they are when they are dry and driving recklessly can easily cost you your life. When it is snowing or raining and you have to drive on the roads, it is recommended that that you lower your speed limit five to ten miles per hour below posted speed limits when it's raining and ten to fifteen miles per hour when it's snowing.

- Make sure your vehicle is safe to drive on the road by submitting daily defect reports. Not having properly working lights, having tyres that are too worn, having a broken windshield and having bad brakes are just a few vehicle ailments that can cause injury to either you or another vehicle or driver. Not having a safe vehicle can cost you a lot of money in fines as well.

Dealing with Injuries

In the event of an incident, you can do a number of things to help, even if you have had no training.

- Further collisions and fire are the main dangers following a crash. Approach any vehicle involved with care. Switch off all engines and, if possible, warn other traffic. Stop anyone from smoking.
- Try to get the assistance of bystanders. Get someone to call the appropriate emergency services as soon as possible. They will need to know the exact location of the incident and the number of vehicles involved.
- DO NOT move casualties still in vehicles unless further danger is threatened. DO NOT remove a motorcyclist's helmet unless it is essential. Remember the casualty may be suffering from shock. DO NOT give them anything to eat or drink. DO try to make them warm and as comfortable as you can, but avoid unnecessary movement. DO give reassurance confidently and try not to leave them alone or let them wander into the path of other traffic.
- Provide emergency care.

Remember the letters D, R, A, B, C

D - Danger - check that you are not in danger.

R - Response - try to get a response by asking questions and gently shaking their shoulders.

A - Airway - the airway should be clear and kept open. Place one hand on the forehead, two fingers under the chin and gently tilt the head back.

B - Breathing - normal breathing should be established. Once the airway is open check breathing for up to 10 seconds.

C - Compressions - if they are not breathing normally compressions should be administered to maintain circulation; place two hands in the centre of the chest and press down 4-5 cms at a rate of 100/ minute. You may only need one hand for a child. Give 30 chest compressions. Then tilt the head back gently, pinch the casualty's nostrils together and place your mouth over theirs. Give two breaths, each lasting one second (use gentle breaths for a small child).

- If the casualty is unconscious and breathing, place them in the recovery position until medical help arrives.
- Bleeding. If there is nothing embedded in a wound, such as glass, apply firm pressure over the wound. Take care not to press on anything that is embedded - build up padding on either side of it. Fasten a pad to the wound with a bandage or length of cloth. Use the cleanest material available. If a limb is bleeding, but not broken, raise it above the level of the heart to reduce the flow of blood. Any restriction of blood circulation for more than a short time could cause long-term injuries.
- Burns. Try to cool the burn by dousing it with clean, cold

water or similar non-toxic liquid for at least ten minutes. Do not try to remove anything sticking to the burn.

• Always carry a first aid kit. You could save a life by learning emergency aid and first aid from a qualified organisation, such as the local ambulance services, the St John Ambulance Association and Brigade, St Andrew's Ambulance Association, the British Red Cross or any suitable qualified body.

What to do if an Accident involves Hazardous Materials
You need to identify the actual properties of the material involved, so that the proper authorities can be notified to deal with the accident, normally the Fire Brigade. They have a procedure chart to assist with this identification so that the correct response may be made.

How to find out more information

Different Methods

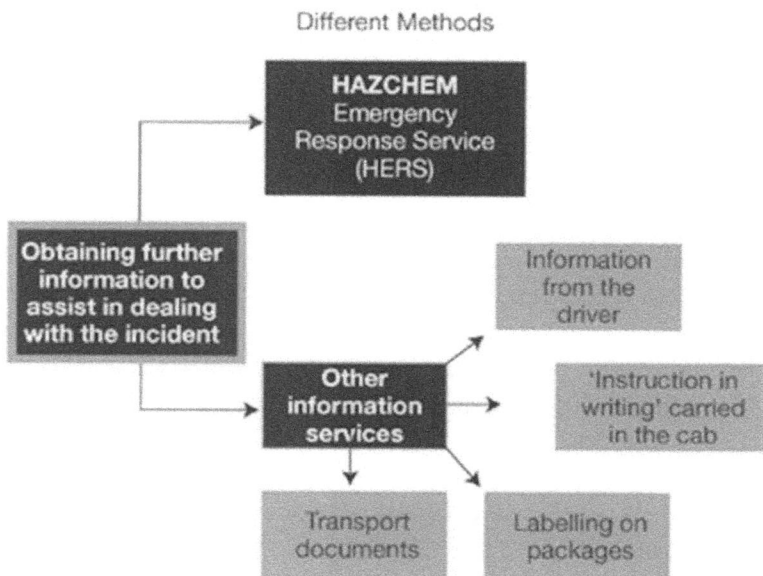

78

Incidents which involve dangerous goods are led by the Fire and Rescue Service (FRS), and are handed over to the Police or Traffic Officer Service when the scene is safe. However, there are occasions when other responders will arrive at the incident scene first. In these circumstances, and only if it is safe to do so, it is important to provide information on the nature of the load being carried to the Fire Service so that the correct equipment and resources can be deployed to the scene. When approaching a scene responders should be careful of any spillages. It is important to consider that any casualties may be a result of the spillage and not of the road traffic collision, so maintaining a safe distance is essential.

S	Survey
A	Assess
D	Disseminate
C	Casualties
H	Hazards
A	Access
L	Location
E	Emergency Services
T	Type
S	Safety

Apart from obvious basic measures, such as taking immediate measures to safeguard yourself and members of the public including other road users, there is a protocol called SAD CHALETS. Using this protocol will ensure that appropriate measures are taken to deal with Hazardous Material accidents.

How to Deal with Casualties

Assess the situation:

- What has happened?
- Is there any further danger to you or the casualty? (roadsides are particularly dangerous places to treat a casualty.)
- How many people are injured?
- Is anybody else able to help?

Assess the casualty:

- What is wrong with the casualty?
- Is it necessary to move them, or can they be left safely in their current position? Remember, further injuries can be caused through unnecessary movement of the casualty.
- Do you need assistance?
- Do you need assistance from the emergency services?
- Don't forget, other first aiders/bystanders can help you.

When you ask for help from the emergency services they will need to know:

- the precise location of the incident
- what happened
- the injuries involved
- how many people are injured

Make a diagnosis:

- What happened to the casualty? Did they fall, faint or have a bump on the head?
- Look for signs such as bleeding, swelling or unaligned limbs.
- If the casualty is conscious, ask them where they feel pain or if they went dizzy before the accident.

Priorities:
The priorities of first aid are usually referred to as the 'ABC of first aid':

- Airway - Check inside the mouth and remove any visible obstruction. Put your fingertips under the point of the casualty's chin. Lift the chin to open the airway.
- Breathing - Spend at least ten seconds looking, listening and feeling for breathing. If the casualty is breathing, put him/her in the recovery position. Continue to monitor the patient's breathing.
- Circulation - Look, listen and feel for normal breathing, coughing or movement by the victim. Only if you have been trained to do so, check the carotid pulse.

Priorities of general treatment (the three B's):

- Breathing (see above).
- Bleeding. Stop bleeding by raising the injured limb above the heart. Apply pressure to the wound with pad, bandage, clean handkerchief or towel.
- Bones. If necessary, immobilise a broken arm in a sling. If a broken leg is suspected, keep the casualty still.

Whilst you are waiting for the arrival of the emergency services:

- Look for changes in the casualty's condition, monitoring the vital signs.
- Check that your treatment is adequate and successful.
- Cooperate with the emergency services when they arrive.

Reporting Accidents

If an accident occurs and you are driving, then you need to assess the situation and see if any of the following situations apply:

- Is anyone (other than yourself) injured?
- Has there been any damage caused to someone else's property, or another vehicle?
- Has an animal (other than any you were transporting in your vehicle) been killed or injured (for these purposes an animal applies to a dog, pig, goat, sheep, ass, mule, horse or cattle).

If any of the above points do apply, you are legally required to stop at the scene and remain there for a reasonable period of time that will allow any people involved directly or indirectly in the accident to come to you and request your contact details. If you are approached by anyone who has reasonable grounds for requesting your information (someone involved with the accident, or who owns property that has been damaged) then you must supply to them your contact details (name and address) and the contact details of the registered owner.

If you don't leave your details at the scene, then you must report the incident to a police officer or at a police station as soon as is practically possible – and in any event, within twenty-fours hours. You can ring to advise the station that you are coming to report a road traffic accident, but it is not acceptable to report the incident over the telephone – it must be done in person. If there is injury caused to another person as a result of the accident, then you are legally required to produce the vehicle insurance certificate, if available, at the scene of the accident if anyone with reasonable grounds requests to see it. If you do not do this at the scene then you must report it to a police station or to a police officer (in person) within twenty-four hours and you must take your insurance certificate with you. If for any reason you do not have your certificate when reporting the incident at the police station, then you must return to the station with it within seven days of the accident.

Take photographs if possible. It is worth carrying a disposable camera in your vehicle at all times in case you end up having an accident. However, many mobile phones have cameras too, so use one if you can - but do make sure you are not breaching any laws by using it while in control of the vehicle.

Information to record:

- The date and time that the accident took place.
- Vehicle details - registration number, make and model of vehicle, colour, any distinguishing features, how many passengers were travelling in the vehicles involved.
- It is also worth asking if anyone involved in the accident is driving a company vehicle, or is driving on company time. If so, get their employer's details too.
- Weather, light conditions and visibility, anything that may have affected driving ability.
- Damage to all vehicles.
- Injuries to any passengers.
- Details of any police officers who attend.

You will need to notify your company with details of the accident, the damage if any to your vehicle and the load and fill in an accident report.

Carrying out Safety Checks, particularly on Brakes, Steering and Tyres to ensure the Vehicle is in a Safe and Legal Condition
Use these important key points to maintain your vehicle in a roadworthy condition.

- Undertake a daily walkaround check, preferably immediately before a vehicle is used.
- First-use inspections are also essential for operators who lease, hire or borrow vehicles. These are especially important where vehicles and trailers have been off the road for some time.
- You as a driver must be able to report promptly any defects or symptoms of defects that could adversely affect the safe operation of vehicles. Reports must be recorded and provision should be made to record details of any rectification and work done.
- Drivers' defect reports, used to record any faults, must be kept for at least fifteen months.
- Safety inspections must include those items covered by the appropriate Department for Transport annual test, including brakes, steering and tyres.
- Safety inspections should be pre-planned, preferably using a time-based programme.
- The system of safety inspections must be regularly monitored, especially in the early stages.
- Any remedial work carried out as a result of safety inspections must be recorded.

The safety inspection record must include:

- Name of owner/operator
- date of inspection

- vehicle identity
- odometer (mileage recorder) reading, if appropriate
- a list of all the items to be inspected
- details of any defects
- name of inspector
- details of any remedial/rectification or repair work and by whom it was done
- statement that any defects have been repaired satisfactorily.

On some types of vehicles and operations, intermediate safety checks may be necessary. Records of safety inspections must be kept for at least fifteen months. Staff carrying out safety inspections must be competent to assess the significance of defects. Assistance must be available to operate the vehicle controls as necessary.

There must be an internal system to ensure that unroadworthy vehicles are removed from service. Understanding the Legal Requirements about Vehicles being kept Safe and Roadworthy. Drivers of vehicles have a legal responsibility to ensure that the vehicles they use are maintained in a safe and roadworthy condition at all times. It is an offence to use an unroadworthy vehicle on the road. Overloading and braking defects are in the top five of the most common Graduated Fixed Penalty (GFP) offences.

In addition to the driver receiving an on-the-spot fine and possible penalty points, GFPs also have an influence on the Operators' Compliance Risk Score (OCRS) - and a poor score is likely to result in an operator being called to a public inquiry before a Traffic Commissioner to explain themselves. This could result in loss of the Operator Licence and of course the loss of the driver's employment When it comes to ensuring the roadworthiness of a vehicle, daily checks are vital in ensuring the safety and reliability of your vehicle. A daily walk-round vehicle check provides a straightforward means for drivers - who are in closest contact with the vehicle and the most likely to be first aware of a problem - to inform the operator that some aspect of the vehicle may be faulty, or in need of repair or replacement. The checks need to be carried out before the vehicle sets out on its journey to make sure it is fit for the road.

Checks should include the external condition ensuring in particular that the following are serviceable:

- lights
- tyres
- wheel fixings
- bodywork
- trailer coupling
- load
- ancillary equipment

This daily check is not meant to be an in-depth inspection of everything. However easily spotted faults should be picked up and rectified BEFORE the vehicle goes out. This is not only important from a compliance point of view, but also for the driver's own health and safety.

The Effects of Windy Weather, particularly Crosswinds, on High-sided Vehicles

High-sided vehicles are most affected by windy weather, but strong gusts can also blow a car, cyclist, motorcyclist or horse rider off course. This can happen on open stretches of road exposed to strong crosswinds, or when passing bridges or gaps in hedges. In very windy weather your vehicle may be affected by turbulence created by large vehicles. Motorcyclists are particularly affected, so keep well back from them when they are overtaking a high-sided vehicle.

The Use of Air Deflectors to Reduce Wind Resistance and Improve Fuel Consumption

Correctly adjusted air deflectors will save fuel. Many articulated tractor units have adjustable roof mounted air deflectors. This is because, over time, the unit will probably be coupled to trailers of varying heights. The roof mounted air deflector should be adjusted to guide airflow over the highest point at the front of the trailer or load. As a rule of thumb, remember that for every ten centimetres of the front of the trailer exposed to airflow, the fuel consumption will worsen by 0.1 mile per gallon (mpg).

HOW TO PASS MODULE 2

Module 2 consists of simple case studies where once more you will be presented with a range of answers from which to choose the correct one, or ones, as some have more than one appropriate answer. Providing you read the introduction to each scenario you will find the questions fairly obvious and you should be able to answer them without too much trouble. The case studies are based on typical real life scenarios that you may encounter as a professional driver.Below is a list of topics which are likely to be covered by the scenarios. You will have covered these topics in Module 1 and the knowledge and understanding you have from that module, together with your own knowledge gained from driving experience, should make it straightforward for you.

- Driving techniques
- Safe and fuel-efficient driving (SAFED)
- Passenger safety
- Dealing with passengers
- Regulations that govern drivers' hours and tachographs
- Regulations that govern the carrying of passengers
- Health and safety at work, both in the workplace and on the road
- Keeping fit for the job

- Dealing with emergencies
- The role of the driver within the company / organisation
- Vehicle controls, equipment and components
- Behaviour on the road
- Vehicle characteristics
- Road and weather conditions
- Traffic signs, rules and regulations
- Vehicle control and procedure
- Motorway driving, Eco-safe driving, Driving techniques
- Safe and Fuel-Efficient driving
- Load safety, Securing of loads, Types of loads
- Vehicle maintenance, Paperwork, The affects of alcohol
- Regulations governing the carriage of illegal immigrants
- Regulations that govern drivers' hours and tachographs
- Health and safety at work, Driver health, Dealing with emergencies
- The role of the driver within the company / organisation
- Freight transport organisation

The case studies part of the Initial Driver CPC qualification will last for 90 minutes. During that time you are required to review 7 different case studies, each with between 5 and 10 questions attached to them. You need to answer 50 questions in total and you need to answer 38 questions correctly to pass. You will use a visual computer monitor similar to the one used for the Multiple Choice and Hazard Perception tests. You will need to use the mouse to guide and click on certain answers.

A practice Case Study is shown at the start of the actual test to allow you to familiarise yourself with how the test is conducted. You will be told the result of the test within 10 minutes of its completion.

SAMPLE CASE STUDIES

CASE STUDY 1

Gary's work today is to make deliveries driving a rigid lorry.
He starts work at 6.30am and the weather is very cold at -4°C.
Gary had little rest and sleep last night as his next door neighbours had a very noisy all night party.
He notices that as he starts the lorry smoke from the exhaust seems as though it is darker than normal.
Today he will deliver to mainly country areas.
Gary is fully aware it is important that his deliveries arrive on time.

Question 1

How can Gary make sure his vehicle is as environmentally friendly as possible?
Select TWO of the options below.

A. Regularly check his vehicle, report all defects and ensure the defects are rectified.
B. Take less time to make his deliveries by driving faster.
C. Note excessive exhaust smoke.
D. Switch the engine off when in heavy traffic queues.

Answer: A, C

Question 2

Why does Gary need to drive slower around corners on the country roads this morning?

Select TWO of the options below.
  A.   There will be heavy traffic jams.
  B.   He could lose control if driving at normal speed around corners.
  C.   Not driving slower, he might hit a kerb and so cause a tyre to burst.
  D.   That early in the morning he may encounter slow moving vehicles, such as tractors.

Answer: B, D

Question 3

Gary is running late with his deliveries.
What should he do?
Select the BEST option below.

  A.   Increase his speed as much as possible.
  B.   Call customers on his mobile while he is driving to explain his lateness.
  C.   Carry on as calmly and safely as possible, understanding that he cannot change the situation.
  D.   Be irritated by the situation, as this will help him concentrate.

Answer: C

Question 4

While Gary has stopped for his break a customer calls him on his mobile phone. The customer is angry and demands to know why his

delivery is late and exactly when it will arrive.
How should Gary respond to the customer's call?
Select the BEST option below.

    A. Be polite and accurately explain the situation, regarding the delay, and when he expects to make the delivery.
    B. Ignore the call and switch off his phone.
    C. Respond that he is the driver and does not deal with customers.
    D. Say he is not far away, even though it is not true.

Answer: A

CASE STUDY 2

Jenny drives an articulated lorry. She will be making deliveries in North Wales. Some of the area is quite steep with narrow roads. She has a co-driver.
Jenny is aware of maintenance costs and is expected by her employer to keep costs down.
Today's deliveries will be on roads that can be busy with tourists, coaches, cyclists and pedestrians.

Question 1

Jenny makes a delivery and notices a rear tyre has burst.
What should Jenny do?
Select the BEST option below.

    A. There is no need to do anything. The other rear tyres on that side of the semi-trailer are still able to operate on their own.

B. Resume her schedule but not over 40mph. Report this when back at the depot.
C. Report it and wait for a replacement to be fitted.
D. Carry on and drive as normal, report when back at depot.

Answer: C

Question 2

Why would Jenny make more use of the retarder today than she usually would expect to?
Select TWO of the options below.

A. The heavy traffic may cause her to drive slower.
B. Normal braking performance reduced on the steeper roads.
C. Save maintenance costs by reducing wear on brake linings.
D. Increase fuel economy driving uphill.
E. Reduce CO_2 emissions by saving on gear changes.

Answer: B, E

Question 3

Jenny's co-driver is ill, which might be a serious asthma attack. Obviously very concerned, Jenny contacts base.
What do they tell her to do?
Select the BEST option below.

A. Drive to the next town and wait for an ambulance.
B. Carry on to the next town and drop the co-driver off.
C. Stay where they are, call for an ambulance and while waiting ask if anybody nearby has medical training.
D. Find a bystander, leave the co-driver with them and carry on with deliveries.
E. See if there is anything useful in the first-aid box.

Answer: C

Question 4

As she drives up into the hills it becomes very misty and visibility is poor.
What safety precautions can Jenny take?
Select TWO of the options below.

A. Stay close to the vehicle in front to so she can see it at all times.
B. Keep checking the speedometer for her accurate speed.
C. Do not increase speed if the mist appears to be clearing.
D. Speed up if a vehicle appears to be close behind.
E. Decrease speed and drive slower.

Answer: B, E

Question 5

Jenny must make extra use of the nearside mirrors today.
Why?

Select TWO of the options below.

A. To ensure she safely passes cyclists and pedestrians.
B. To always check at that cyclists or pedestrians have are not between the kerb and the front nearside wheel at junctions.
C. To check for vehicles overtaking her on the narrow roads.
D. To see if it is clear to pull out.
E. The offside mirror is missing.

Answer: A, B

Question 6

Jenny needs to reverse the lorry into a parking space surrounded by other lorries, coaches and tourists.
What should she do?
Select TWO of the options that she could follow.

A. Ask one of the tourists to guide her into the space.
B. Find a responsible person to help her.
C. Park the lorry by herself using the horn and audible reversing alarm.
D. Physically get out of the lorry and tell people she is about to reverse into the space and ask them to stand clear.

Answer: C, D

Question 7

Why does Jenny have to be aware of the width of her lorry?

Select TWO of the options below.

A. So she can squeeze past other vehicles, cyclists and pedestrians.
B. It is likely she will meet oncoming traffic on narrow and busy roads.
C. If she knocked and broke the offside mirror on another vehicle it would make her lorry unroadworthy
D. If there are low bridges.

Answer: B, D

CASE STUDY 3

Dave is driving a heavily laden rigid lorry. It has been raining on and off throughout the day and is now turning to light snow.
On today's route there are many sharp bends and mini roundabouts. The town centre has traffic calming measures and there is a hump back bridge on the approach to the city.
Dave comes across an accident where there are injured people.

Question 1

How can Dave maintain control of his vehicle in these conditions? Select TWO of the options below.

A. Brake when driving around bends.
B. Increase acceleration quickly after roundabouts.
C. Always brake in good time.
D. Brake when travelling in a straight line.

E.   Just before a bend, he should brake.

Answer: C, D

Question 2

Dave has always carries drinks with him.
Of the following, which drinks will most easily keep Jacob hydrated?
Select THREE of the options below.

A.   Tea
B.   Coffee
C.   Bottled water
D.   Alcohol
E.   Tap Water
F.   Sugar-free caffeine (such as cola)

Answer: A, C, E

Question 3

Dave arrives at an accident site where an injured person has burns.
What should Dave do?
Select THREE of the options below.

A.   He should call for an ambulance.
B.   Remove anything sticking to the burns.
C.   He should not attempt to remove anything sticking to the burns.
D.   Look for clean, cold and non-toxic fluids with which to put

on the burns.

Answer: A, C, D

Question 4

Why should Dave be especially aware of the length of his lorry?
Select THREE of the options below.

A. There are narrow roads in the town centre.
B. His lorry may overhang kerbs and verges when turning the vehicle.
C. Mini roundabouts are on his route.
D. His route may take him under low bridges.
E. His lorry could ground on hump back bridges.

Answer: A, B, E

CASE STUDY 4

Eric's work today is to make deliveries driving a 3.5 tonne parcel delivery van.
He starts work at 7.30am and the weather is mild at 14 degrees.
He has a very busy day ahead of multi drop parcels.

Question 1

While he is doing his walkaround check, he stops when he notices that there is a slight leak of what appears to be diesel fuel coming from under the engine compartment.

He reports this to the mechanic, who makes a quick repair with insulating tape and says it 'should' be ok. Eric is unsure that the leak has been effectively repaired.

How should Eric deal with this situation?

Select the BEST option below.

A. Accept that the mechanic should know best and drive away to start making deliveries, then remember to check again the following morning.

B. Write a defect report and point it out to a more senior member of staff for a second opinion.

C. Put extra tape around the repair to strengthen the mechanic's work.

D. Decide to deal with it when he gets back as making deliveries on time is so important, but make occasional checks when he stops in case it has worsened.

Answer: B

Question 2

Eric is running late today, like most days. As usual he has not time for anything other than two hot dogs and a paper cup of coffee at a roadside cafe. He is beginning to experience stomach acidity and a general feeling of unwellness.

How should he deal with this situation?

Select the BEST option below.

A. Accept that acidity and upset stomach is normal for

professional drivers who have little opportunity for adequate diet and exercise.

B. Tell his employer that he needs to take a longer lunch break to give him a chance to sit in a transport cafe for his favourite meal of bacon, eggs and fried bread.

C. Take the trouble to pack a healthy lunch with him that includes fruit and fibre as well as the other ingredients of a healthy lifestyle. Wash it down with bottled water if nothing else is available.

Answer: C

Question 3

Eric had just made a delivery to the Port of Dover. As he is driving away from Dover, he hears strange sounds coming from the back of his van, he suspects someone may be hiding in there.
How should he deal with this situation?
Select the BEST option below.

A. Suspecting illegal immigrants are hiding amidst his load, he uses his mobile phone while driving to call police, so that the suspects do not have a chance to escape until the police arrive.

B. Stop his vehicle and make a visual check of the load to see if immigrants or criminals are hiding there, so that he can call the police if he detects anyone.

C. Having good grounds to suspect illegal immigrants, stops his vehicle and phones the police to request that they come

to him and check his vehicle.
D.   Negotiate a fee to take them to a major city.
E.   Stop the vehicle and physically eject anyone hiding there.

Answer: C

Question 4

Eric is on the last drop of the day and running late when he realises that his speed limiter is not working. He only has the one drop to make and can then return to the depot where it can be fixed.
How should he deal with the situation?
Select the BEST option below.

A.   Be thankful that he can keep the customer happy by making the drop on and get back to the depot before it closes. He can then report the defect.
B.   Stop and contact his depot and report the fault for it to be repaired before he can continue.
C.   Appreciate that speed limiters are there for a purpose and make sure he does not exceed the normal limit set by the speed limiter. Report the fault on return to the depot.
D.   Do nothing, speed limiters are a nuisance that waste valuable time.

Answer: B

CASE STUDY 5

Raymond is driving a heavily laden articulated lorry. The weather is very cold, it has been raining and there is some risk of ice. Visibility is quite poor.

Question 1

When Raymond stops mid-morning to offload part of his load, he notices that one of his rear lights is not working.
How should Raymond best deal with this situation?
Select the BEST option below.

A. Decide that he still has one rear light working and it is more important to get urgent deliveries completed, so he carries on.

B. Contact his depot, report the fault and ask for it to be attended to immediately in view of the poor driving visibility.

C. Drive faster to get back to the depot before nightfall so that technically he does not have to use his rear lights.

Answer: B

Question 2

Raymond is increasingly concerned at worsening driving conditions. As well as poor visibility, the roads look icy. He is concerned to complete his day's work before the weather closes in completely.

There is a shortcut along country lanes that he could take, it is quite legal for his vehicle.
How should Raymond best deal with this situation?
Select the BEST option below.

A.   Take the short cut, his employer and customers will be pleased that he has taken the initiative and got the deliveries completed on time.
B.   Continue along the normal route, which is main roads and motorways, knowing that these types of roads are gritted early when conditions are icy.
C.   Use a combination of country and motorway routes to get there in the quickest time.

Answer: B

Question 3

During the journey, the windscreen washer fluid freezes.
How should Raymond deal with this situation?
Select the BEST option below.

A.   Stop and wipe the screen clean when it gets too dirty for safe vision.
B.   Contact his employers for advice on de-icing the washer mechanism, advising them of any nearby garages that may stock windscreen de-icing fluid.
C.   Continue on as everyone is using their lights and he can see oncoming vehicles quite easily.
D.   Soak a rag in radiator antifreeze solution and wipe it over the windscreen.

Answer: B

Question 4

During the journey, whilst on a narrow two way road, an oncoming heavy lorry smashes his driver's wing mirror.
How should he deal with this situation?
Select the BEST option below.

A.   Immediately stop in a safe place and report the situation to his depot.
B.   Ignore it, the lorry that damaged his mirror has disappeared and nothing is to be gained by making himself late.
C.   Take the vanity mirror from the passenger sun visor and tape it to the metal mirror support as a temporary expedient, so that his deliveries can be made on time.
D.   Turn his vehicle around and give chase to the lorry that damaged his mirror so as to make a compensation claim.

Answer: A

HOW TO PASS MODULE 3

You will need to undertake a practical driving test in the LGV of your choice. This will include an Eco-Safe Driving assessment which does not contribute to the result of the test.

Eco Safe Driving Guidance
(See http://www.youtube.com/dsagov#p/a/u/0/DVLN1IKA7YU)

This is assessed during the test but is not marked towards a pass or fail.

- Use anticipation to maintain momentum and reduce fuel usage.
- Use gears in an effective and fuel efficient manner.
- Use acceleration sense to improve fuel economy.
- Use additional braking/retarder systems effectively.
- Minimise the effects of drag.
- Reduce the economic impact of air-con use.
- Know what and how to check their vehicle for optimum efficiency.

You should note that poor fuel efficiency is often a result of erratic driving behaviour and is characterised by harsh braking and rapid acceleration. Eco Safe Driving develops driver hazard perception and promotes smart, smooth and safer driving techniques. These driving techniques are realistic and when applied correctly will allow the driver and fleet manager to benefit from on-going fuel-savings and improved CO_2 emissions.

Vehicle Safety Questions
At the beginning of the test, you will be asked some vehicle safety questions.

Practical Driving and Off-road Exercises
You will be examined on your practical road driving ability and some off-road exercises. The test will last about 90 minutes.

The off-road exercises will include:
- an 'S' shaped reverse into a bay
- demonstrating the uncoupling and re-coupling procedure if you're taking a test with a trailer

During your practical road driving, the examiner will observe how you:

- use the vehicle controls
- move away at an angle, uphill and downhill
- conduct a braking exercise
- use the mirrors
- give appropriate signals
- show awareness and anticipation of other road users intentions
- manage your progress and control your vehicle speed
- deal with hazards
- select a safe place to stop

Basic Vehicle Checks
Firstly you must demonstrate a knowledge of the necessary vehicle checks.

- Condition & function of seat belts
- Head restraint adjustment
- Mirror adjustment
- Tax disk
- First aid kit
- Fire extinguisher
- Torch
- Warning triangle
- Vehicle handbook
- Warning light
- All lights
- Horn
- Washers & wipers
- Brake
- Fuel
- Engine oil level
- Coolant level
- Windscreen wash level
- Brake/clutch fluid
- Power steering fluid
- Condition of battery
- Oil or waste leaks
- Condition of vehicle bodywork, windscreen, windows, lights
- Condition of windscreen wiper blades
- Cleanness of windscreen, windows, mirrors, lights, number plate
- Security of load, trailer, roof rack
- Condition of tyres, tyre pressure, tyre wear

- Availability of spare wheel & jack

Note: You should also refer to the Driver Walkaround Chart in the appendices at the back of this book.

Actual on-road driving time for all C (rigid) categories will be a minimum of one hour. You will need to answer approximately five questions on basic vehicle checks. You will also have to demonstrate your ability to reverse into a marked bay. There will be a controlled brake test. Test may also include hill starts and motorway driving.

The test will take an hour and a half, with at least an hour of driving. The examiner will assess your driving in a variety of traffic conditions, and on several different types of road. Your practical driving test will include approximately ten minutes of independent driving. This is designed to test your ability to drive unsupervised, and make safe decisions without guidance. During your test you'll have to drive independently by either following traffic signs, a series of directions OR a combination of both.

Independent driving is not a test of your orientation and navigation skills, or your ability to remember directions. Driving independently means making your own decisions. This includes deciding when it is safe and appropriate to ask for confirmation about where you are going. To help you understand where you are going, the examiner may show you a diagram.

If you go off the route or take a wrong turning, the examiner will help you to get back on the route and continue with the independent driving. Going off the driving route will not affect your result unless you commit a driving fault. You will not need to have a detailed knowledge of the area. You cannot use a Sat Nav for independent driving as it gives you turn-by-turn prompts.

The practical test is made up of two parts.
The first part is at the test centre.

REVERSING EXERCISE

Starting with the front of the vehicle in line with the two marker cones A, reverse into the bay, keeping marker B on the offside and stop with the extreme rear of the vehicle within the 75 centimetre stopping area.

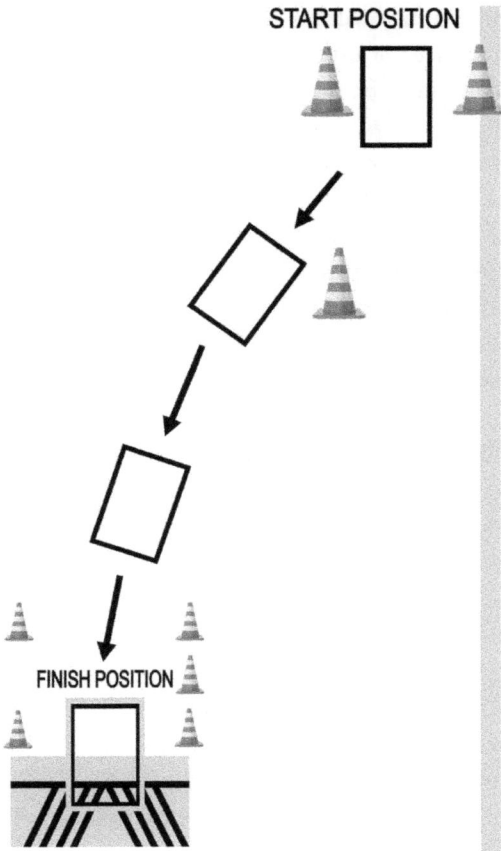

Distance between cones A = 1.5 times the width of the vehicle.

Distance from cones A to cone B = 2 times the length of the vehicle.

Distance from cone B to point D = 3 times the length of the vehicle.

The width of the bay (C) will be 1.5 times the width of the vehicle. The length of the bay will be either the length of the vehicle, or 3 ft longer, 3ft shorter or 6ft shorter at the examiner's discretion. The precise length will not be disclosed in advance.

The manoeuvring area should be set at 92.5 metres in length to accommodate vehicles up to 18.5 metres long. For vehicles greater in length and up to 18.75 metres, the two cones A should be set on the yellow line and be twice the length of the vehicle combination. Cone B should be set two vehicle lengths away. This will have the effect that these larger vehicles will manoeuvre in an area less than five times the actual length of the vehicle combination.

Controlled Brake Test

For this exercise, you will be required to drive forward approximately 200ft to reach approximately 20mph. You must brake after passing marker cones A, stopping as quickly as possible, with safely and under full control. The stopping area will have a solid yellow line and a black hatched section. There will also be a barrier at the end of the reversing bay, and the vehicle must stop with its rear inside the 75 centimetre wide yellow and black stopping area.

The second part of the test takes place on public roads. It may include driving on motorways, depending on where you take your test. You will have to carry out exercises specific to the type of vehicle you drive. For example, if you are driving a bus or a coach, you will be asked to stop at a bus stop and move away when the examiner tells you to.

The practical test also includes an eco-safe driving assessment which involves the examiner taking note of how you control the vehicle and plan your driving. This assessment does not count towards the result of the test, however the examiner will give you feedback at the end of your test.

Traffic Signs

Note: there is a free online traffic sign test ite at:
http://www.driving-test-success. com/theory/test002/test002.htm

Lists of UK road signs and markings can be downloaded from:

http://www.direct.gov.uk/ en/TravelAndTransport/ Highwaycode/Signsandmarkings/ index.htm

A complete list of UK traffic signs can be downloaded from: http://webarchive.nationalarchives.gov.uk/+/http://www.dft.gov. uk/pgr/roads/tss/trafficsigns.pdf

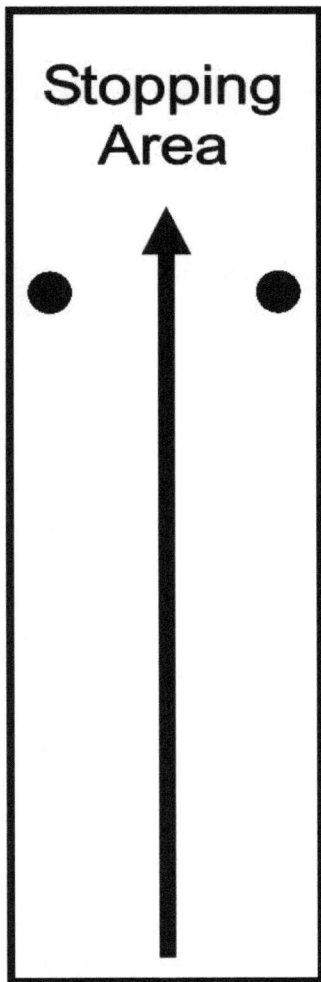

The Highway Code has a list of the relevant signs too. A few helpful notes about road signs in the UK

Directional Signs

The term "directional sign" covers both Advance Direction Signs (ADS), placed on the approach to a junction, and Direction Signs (DS) at the junction itself, showing where to turn. ADS has a chevron (pointed) end, and this type is also referred to as a flag-type sign.

An Advance Direction Sign may be one of four types:

- Stack type — with the destinations in each direction on a separate panel that also contains an arrow
- Map-type — to give a highly clear and simplified diagrammatic plan view of a junction, for example a roundabout
- Dedicated lane — shows the destinations separated by vertical dotted lines to indicate which lane to use
- Mounted overhead — for use on busy motorways and other wide roads where verge mounted signs would be frequently obstructed by other traffic

An ADS generally has blue, green or white as its background colour to indicate the status of road (motorway, primary or non-primary) on which it is placed. Except on the main carriageway of a motorway, coloured panels are used to indicate routes from the junction being signed that have a different status. ADS should always be a single colour indicating the status of the road to be joined, although there are a few rare exceptions to this rule. All types of ADS (but not DS) may optionally have the junction name at the top of the sign in capital letters in a separate panel.

A route confirmatory sign is placed either after a junction where distances were not shown on the ADS or DS or is placed on an overhead information sign but does not show distances to the destinations along that route.

Warning Signs

The importance of a warning sign is emphasised by the red border drawn around it and the mostly triangular shape. This sign warns drivers that there may be a queue (line) of traffic ahead, possibly hidden beyond a visual obstruction.

Regulatory Signs

Signs in circular red borders are prohibitive, whether or not they also have a diagonal red line. Circular blue signs mainly give a positive (mandatory) instruction. Such circular signs may be accompanied by, or place on, a rectangular plate (information) that provides details of the prohibition or instruction; for example, waiting and loading plates and zone entry signs.

"Stop" signs (octagonal) and "Give Way" signs (inverted triangle) are the two notable exceptions, the distinctive shapes being recognisable even if the face is obscured by dirt or snow.

Informational Signs

Informational signs are mainly rectangular (square or oblong) but, strictly speaking, this category also covers directional signs. They are often coloured to match the directional signing for the status of road in question, but where this is not necessary they are generally blue with white text. Examples include "lane gain" and "lane drop" signs on grade-separated roads, and "IN" and "OUT" indications for accesses to private premises from the highway.

Roadworks Signs

Roadworks are normally signalled with a triangular, red-bordered warning format and are used to indicate that there are works ahead. The graphic is of a man digging. Within the roadworks, diversions and other instructions to drivers are normally given on yellow signs with black script.

ON THE ROAD – THE TEST

Finally, when you are undertaking the test itself, remember that you are driving as you would on your original LGV or even car driving test. If you wish to pass easily, practice this careful method of driving in your day-to-day driving so that it comes as second nature during the test. Your objective is to pass the driving part of the Driver CPC, not show how clever you are at taking shortcuts. Drive carefully and considerately and make the examiner feel comfortable and safe.

Here are links to some helpful government videos online:

http://www.youtube.com/watch?v=w4GfZ0_Klys

http://www.youtube.com/watch?v=CRugJOvV06w

http://www.youtube.com/watch?v=ln0g-JLmDbs

http://www.youtube.com/watch?v=AURXQf4k5gY&feature=channel

HOW TO PASS MODULE 4

One of the commonest causes of failure in Module 4 is being faced with something unexpected that you have not prepared for. You need to practice the safe loading techniques as well as the other techniques, walkaround, safety, prevention of illegal immigrants etc. So no matter how stupid you may feel at the time, practice doing the things outlined here and in the various online videos that we point you towards so that you are prepared for anything. That way, you will pass, first time. During the test you will be required to demonstrate your knowledge and ability in the areas listed below:

Ability to Load the Vehicle with due Regard for Safety Rules and Proper Vehicle Use. LGV tests will also see the introduction of a new piece of equipment called the 'Load Securing Demonstration Trolley' (LSDT) which will allow you to demonstrate your ability to secure loads using a variety of methods including ropes, chains, straps, etc.

Official demonstration video for the LSDT:

http://www.youtube.com/watch?v=DEKaD7SCoc0&feature=play er_embedded

Load Safety Demonstration Trolley

General Requirements for Securing Loads

The total load restraint system will generally consist of a combination of:

- lashings secured to anchorage points attached to the vehicle chassis, which includes cross bearers, outriggers etc.
- bulking arrangements including headboards, bulkheads, spigots, transverse beams, shoring bars etc. which are securely attached to the vehicle
- friction between the load and the vehicle platform

Vehicles using fabric sides, for example curtainsiders, will normally require additional internal restraints.

In view of the wide diversity of general loads it is not possible to suggest loading methods for all the types of load likely to be encountered. However, the basic precautions outlined above will always be applicable. Vehicles equipped with headboards, tailboards or sideboards, or van bodies will provide some restraint. Additional load restraint will be required under any of the following conditions:

If there is a risk that the load may break through the walls, sideboards or tailboard of the vehicle:

- When the load is higher than the headboard, sideboards or tailboard of the vehicle
- If the load is liable to be damaged should it move during transit
- If there is a risk of the load being blown off, or bouncing out of the vehicle

Loading Arrangements on Vehicles
Two essential requirements must be satisfied when loading vehicles. These are that the load must be distributed so that:

The maximum permitted gross vehicle weight and axle weights are not exceeded, and the load centre of gravity is kept as low as possible to achieve maximum stability when the vehicle is braked, or accelerated or changes direction.

For maximum stability, the items comprising of the total load should be evenly spread to achieve minimum height and be arranged to form a uniform whole so that no excessive stress is applied to whatever restraining devices are used. Where a part of the load is to be picked up or removed during the course of a journey the effect on gross vehicle weight, individual axle weights and on the securing and stability of the load then being carried must be considered during the initial loading and subsequent unloading. For example, removing a part of the load from behind the rear axle of a vehicle or trailer will reduce the gross vehicle weight, but it will increase the weight on the front axles and may cause individual axles to exceed their plated weights.

Principles of Load Safety

The basic principle upon which this Code of Practice is based is that the combined strength of the load restraint system must be sufficient to withstand a force not less than the total weight of the load forward, so as to prevent the load moving under severe braking, and half of the weight of the load backwards and sideways. Vertical movement may occur but this should be overcome if the above conditions are met. This applies to all vehicles no matter what the size, from small vans to the largest goods vehicles. These principles are based on the maximum forces that are likely to be experienced during normal road use. Greater forces may be encountered if the vehicle, for example, is involved in an accident. The principles should therefore be regarded as minimum requirements.

FULL WEIGHT OF LOAD FORWARDS

HALF WEIGHT OF LOAD SIDEWAYS

FULL WEIGHT OF LOAD REARWARDS

Restraint Equipment

Various types of equipment can be used for restraining general freight loads. These include rope, chains, steel wire rope, webbing, strapping or netting. For the securing of loads inside van bodies and similar load containers, specially designed shoring piles used in conjunction with the appropriate securing fixtures on the vehicle are suitable. Purpose built restraining devices should only be used for the application, and in the manner approved by their manufacturers.

Boxes

Boxes must be loaded so that they are prevented from moving in any direction. They should interlock if possible, and be loaded to a uniform height. There must be at least one lashing for each row of boxes across the vehicle and any box which is above the general height of the load must have at least one cross lashing, more depending on weight and size.

Metals

Small relatively heavy items, such as small castings, if not palletised or caged, should be securely restrained and carried on sided vehicles. The headboard, sideboards, and tailboard must be higher than the load and must be strong enough to withstand the forces generated by the vehicle's motion. Careful attention should be paid to points where lashings pass over corners of the load to ensure that the load is not damaged by chain links etc. or that the lashings are damaged by sharp edges. Corner protectors and sleeves should be used whenever necessary.

The friction between individual items in a load will generally be low, particularly if the metal is oiled, and should therefore be disregarded when assessing the total load restraint required. The friction between load and vehicle platform will also be considerably reduced if either is wet or greasy. The only exception to this rule is when concrete reinforcing weld mesh is carried. In this case there is significant friction between bundles of the mesh loaded on top of each other. A large mass can be restrained more effectively than a number of small items and therefore whenever possible loads should be aggregated into the largest or heaviest unit feasible. This will be controlled to some extent by the facilities available at the point of unloading. Metal loads can take various forms but they can be broadly divided into nine categories:

- Flat Sheet
- Long sections
- Coils
- Large units and castings
- Scrap metal
- Scrap vehicles
- Machinery and tools
- Steel for the Reinforcement of Concrete
- Combination of the above i.e. mixed loads

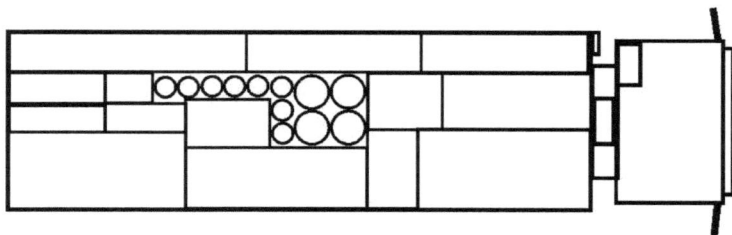

Example of a safely loaded vehicle carrying mixed cargo.

Mixed Loads

When a load is composed of different items each part of the load must be secured in a manner suitable to a load of its type. This applies mainly to cross lashings. The longitudinal lashings must be adequate for the total weight of the load, and separators must be used so that no part of the load can move forward independently.

The following procedures should be followed when applicable:

- Where mixed loads involve heavy solid articles and light crushable boxes, the heavier articles should provide the base and rear part and the light portion be loaded on top and to the front.
- When loading different sizes of container small items should be central, with the larger items forming the outer walls of the load. Avoid as far as possible obstructions or projections beyond the vehicle sides.
- Keep irregular shaped items for the upper part of the load where it is not possible to place them centrally within the load.
- Special precautions may have to be taken when dangerous substances are included in a load. These include segregation of substances which may interact together, protection from rain and careful handling and stowage to reduce the risk of damage to vulnerable containers. The packages should be loaded in such a manner as to enable the labels to be easily read.

There are many types of load other than mentioned above, a list of other load types include:

- Sacks
- Loose Bricks
- Timber
- Pallets
- Bulk liquids, Powders, Grain etc.

Regardless of the load type, they will all require variant forms of restraint and loading in/on the vehicle and the equipment required to ensure full load security in all cases will undoubtedly vary from load to load.

Iso Containers

The majority of containers in use are constructed to International (ISO 1496) or British (BS 3951) standards. A common feature in the construction of these containers is that specially designed corner castings are incorporated which can be used. In conjunction with twist locks fitted on the vehicle, to provide a simple and positive means of restraint.

This type of container should only be carried on vehicles fitted with twist locks. Twist locks must be maintained in serviceable condition and a minimum of four used for each container carried. Provided that the twist locks are fully engaged and locked in position, the container will be adequately secured and no further restraint will be necessary.

The operator is confronted with a number of problems when attempting to carry ISO containers on vehicles not equipped with twist locks. Unlike normal box type loads that spread their weight over a large area, containers are designed to stand on the twist lock sockets or feet that protrude down at each corner. With heavy containers this produces high point loading that could over-stress a normal platform floor. Other platform vehicles may have raised or wide section side ledges which would prevent the container from resting on the platform floor. The resultant interface between the side ledges and the container feet would offer little frictional resistance making it virtually impossible to secure the container on to the vehicle safely and the practice should be avoided.

Security of the Vehicle and Contents

There are considerations that you should be aware of to keep your vehicle and load secure from criminals.

- Remove keys and lock vehicle doors whenever the vehicle is left unattended, even for a second. This includes when paying for fuel, buying a paper, making a delivery or receiving instructions.
- Drive with the doors locked in order to deter thieves who may try to enter the vehicle when it is stationary. If anti-theft systems are fitted, make sure they are working and use them.
- Park overnight at approved locations if possible, and avoid dark, isolated places. Try to park in a way that prevents access to the rear doors.
- If you are asked to re-deliver to a new address, always check with your traffic office first and wait for confirmation before moving on
- Try to travel in convoy with other trusted drivers when delivering high value or vulnerable loads. Be aware of bogus officials (who could be wearing stolen uniforms) or distractions: drivers may be alerted or stopped by 'other drivers' for supposed punctures, accidents, rear shutter insecure or door open, someone seeking help/directions etc. In conjunction with this point, the use of a Vulnerable Load Card is recommended to discourage opportunist bogus thieves. (The card is kept in the driver's cab and states that the driver is instructed not to open his door but is prepared to follow an officer to the police station to do so - it may not stop the professional gang but might deter the opportunist).
- Keep documentation about your load safely tucked out of sight. Do not talk to others about what you're doing, where you are going or what you are carrying.

- If you realise a theft from your vehicle is going on, do not leave the safety of your cab. Lock the doors, start the engine, switch on the lights and if necessary sound the horn to attract attention.
- When returning to an unattended vehicle, always check for signs of tampering with doors, seals, straps or sheets.

Ability to Prevent Criminality and Trafficking in Illegal Immigrants

Drivers should be aware that a penalty of £2,000 is imposed for each illegal immigrant found in their vehicle, with confiscation of the vehicle should the fine not be paid. Anybody aiding illegal immigrants to enter Great Britain could be imprisoned for up to seven years. Proof of 'due diligence' may be accepted in defence of any charges under the legislation, but it is important for an accused driver to clearly show that he followed current Home Office legislation.

Where it is alleged that a person is liable to a penalty under the Immigration Act for bringing a clandestine entrant into the United Kingdom it is a defence to show:

- he did not know and had no reasonable grounds for suspecting that a clandestine entrant was, or might be, concealed in the transporter
- that there was an effective system in operation in relation to the transporter to prevent the carriage of clandestine entrants
- that on the occasion concerned, the person or persons responsible for operating that system did so properly

These are some of the measures you need to have knowledge of in order to secure vehicles against unauthorised entry. Practice taking these measures so that you can show the Driver CPC examiner that you know what you are doing:

- Before final loading takes place, all existing cuts or tears in the outer shell or fabric of the vehicle that exceed 25 centimetres in length must be repaired and sealed so as to prevent unauthorised entry.
- If present at the time of final loading, the driver must check to ensure that no persons have gained entry to the vehicle and are concealed inside. It must then be locked, sealed, or otherwise made secure to prevent unauthorised entry.
- If not present at the time of final loading the driver must, where possible, ensure that such checks are conducted at that point by reputable persons and then obtain written confirmation that these checks were properly conducted and that the vehicle did not contain concealed persons at the time of final loading and securing.
- When the final loading has been completed, the load space must be secured immediately by lock, seal or other security device, preventing unauthorised entry.
- Tilt cords and straps, where used, must be undamaged, pass through all fastening points, be made taut and be secured by lock, seal or other security device.
- There must be no means of entry to the load space, other than via access points that have been secured by lock, tilt cord/strap and seal, or other security device.
- Locks, tilt cords, straps and other devices used to secure the load space must be of robust quality and effective.
- Seals other than Customs' seals must be distinguished by a number from a series that is unique to the owner, hirer or driver. This must be recorded in documentation accompanying the vehicle.
- Where a sealed container (except a container sealed by

Customs) is loaded onto a vehicle, the owner, hirer or driver must, where possible, check to ensure that it does not contain unauthorised persons. It must then be resealed and made secure in accordance with the above requirements. These actions and the number of the new seal used must be recorded in documentation accompanying the vehicle.

- The same checking, securing and recording procedure detailed above must be followed where the load space in the vehicle has been opened by the owner, hirer, driver, or any other person before the final checks detailed below are carried out.
- Where a new driver becomes responsible for the vehicle en route to the United Kingdom, he should ensure that it does not contain unauthorised persons and that the requirements detailed above have all been met.
- If the the owner, hirer or driver does not have the appropriate locks etc they will need to establish alternative arrangements to prevent unauthorised entry, and be able to demonstrate that such arrangements have been made and complied with.

Prior to the vehicle boarding a ship, aircraft or train to the United Kingdom or before arrival at the UK immigration control at Coquelles [ie, the Channel Tunnel terminal]

- Where used, check tilt cords and straps for evidence of tampering, damage or repair.
- Where used, check that seals, locks or other security devices have not been removed, damaged or replaced. In order to ensure that there has been no substitution, numbers on seals must be checked to confirm that they correspond with those recorded on the documentation accompanying the vehicle.
- Check the outer shell/fabric of the vehicle for signs of damage or unauthorised entry, paying particular attention to

the roof, which may be checked from either inside or outside the vehicle.

- Check any external storage compartments, toolboxes, wind deflectors and beneath the vehicle.
- Check inside the vehicle. Effective detection devices may be used for this purpose at the discretion of the owner, hirer or driver, but this will not obviate the requirement that the other checks detailed above be carried out. Where it is not possible to secure a vehicle lock, seal or other security device, a thorough manual check of the load and load space must be conducted.

General Principles

- Vehicles should be checked regularly en route to the United Kingdom to ensure that they have not been entered, particularly after stops when left unattended.
- A document detailing the system operated to prevent unauthorised entry must be carried with the vehicle, so that it may be produced immediately to an immigration officer on demand in the event of possible liability to a penalty.
- A report detailing the checks that were carried out must be carried with the vehicle. If it is possible to arrange, the report should be endorsed by a third party who has either witnessed or carried out the checks himself by arrangement with the owner, hirer or driver, as the report will then be of greater evidential value.
- Whilst owners, hirers or drivers may contract with other persons to carry out the required checks on their behalf, they will nevertheless remain liable to any penalty incurred in the event of failure to have an effective system in place or to operate it properly on the occasion in question.

- Where the checks conducted suggest that the security of the vehicle may have been breached, or the owner, hirer or driver otherwise has grounds to suspect that unauthorised persons have gained entry to the vehicle, it must not be taken on to the ship, aircraft or train embarking for the United Kingdom, or to the UK immigration control at Coquelles. Any such circumstances must be reported to the police in the country concerned at the earliest opportunity, or, at the latest, to the passport control authorities at the port of embarkation. In the event of difficulties arising, owners, hirers or drivers should contact the UK Immigration Service at the proposed port of arrival for advice.

Ability to Assess Emergency Situations

What this means in practice is the measures you would undertake in extreme weather, especially in regard to diesel fuel and driving visual aids, mirrors etc. Also the emergency procedure to adopt if your vehicle catches fire during your journey and be able to identify the various types of fire extinguisher and know which fires they're intended to tackle. You also need to know how to enter and exit your vehicle safely with due regard for other road users and pedestrians.

Ability to Prevent Physical Risk

You will have noted the Drivers Walkaround check sheet at the back of this book. Preventing physical risk means understanding how to carry out the checks on that sheet as well as the simple precautions to be taken before starting the engine.

Following the walkaround check:

- Ensure that you can easily and comfortably reach and operate all the main controls of the vehicle.

- Check that you can take clear observations to the front of the vehicle through the windscreen and to the rear via the mirrors.
- Before starting your engine note whether all the doors are closed.
- Check the mirrors to make sure they are properly adjusted.
- Fasten your seatbelt and make sure that it is not twisted.
- Check the handbrake to see if it is on.
- Check the gear lever to see if it is in neutral.

Emphasis throughout the test will be on you to demonstrate your ability during and after the physical walkaround vehicle safety check.

The test consists of five questions which cover the Driver CPC syllabus. For each of the questions the examiner will require you to demonstrate your knowledge in the syllabus areas mentioned above, which could involve you carrying out actions such as walking round the vehicle pointing out relevant parts of a vehicle, or demonstrating the use of relevant parts of the vehicle.

Each question equals 20% of the overall pass mark. To pass the test an overall score of 80% must be achieved, with a score of at least 15% in each question.

APPENDIX 1 - DRIVER'S DAILY WORKAROUND

Please visit the VOSA website to view the critcally important daily workaround:

http://www.dft.gov.uk/vosa/repository/HGV%20pullout.pdf

APPENDIX 2 - EU RULES ON DRIVER HOURS

The European Union (EU) drivers' hours rules set limits for daily, weekly and fortnightly driving. The rules also specify minimum breaks for drivers during the working day, and daily and weekly rest periods.

The main points of the EU rules are:

- Daily driving must not exceed nine hours, although this may be extended to ten hours twice a week.
- Weekly driving must not exceed 56 hours.
- Fortnightly driving must not exceed 90 hours in any two consecutive weeks.
- Drivers must take breaks that total at least 45 minutes during or after a maximum of 4.5 hours of driving. The break can be split into two periods, one of at least 15 minutes followed by one of at least 30 minutes. You cannot split breaks into three periods of 15 minutes.
- Drivers must normally take at least 11 consecutive hours of daily rest. This can be reduced by up to two hours on no more than three occasions between any two weekly rest periods.
- Drivers may split their daily rest into two periods totalling 12 hours. If they do, the first period must be at least three hours

and the second at least nine hours. You cannot split daily rest into more than two periods.

- Within six 24-hour periods from the end of their last weekly rest, drivers must extend their daily rest period into a weekly rest period. This may be either the regular 45-hour weekly rest or a reduced period of at least 24 hours.

- With effect from 4 June 2010, the weekly rest requirement for drivers on international occasional coach journeys changed. The concession allows drivers on single international journeys to postpone their weekly rest period until the end of the twelfth day. It also requires the driver to take a regular 45-hour rest prior to the journey beginning, in addition to requiring at least one regular and one reduced weekly rest period back-to-back on the journey's completion, which amounts to a minimum rest period of at least 69 hours.

APPENDIX 3 - TACHOGRAPHS

A tachograph is a device that records a vehicle's speed over time. Usually fitted to lorries behind the speedometer, a tachograph records the lorry's speed and whether it is moving or stationary. The mechanical tachograph uses a stylus to plot a line on a moving paper disk that rotates throughout the day, where one rotation encompasses 24 hours. The marker moves further from the centre the faster the vehicle is moving. However, these are vulnerable to tampering, and so are being replaced by electronic tachographs which record data on smart cards.

Tachographs are mandatory for lorries in some jurisdictions and drivers can be required to produce them on demand by transport authorities who are charged with enforcing regulations governing drivers' working hours.

Digital tachographs make tampering much more difficult by sending signals in an encrypted manner. EU regulation 1360/2002 makes digital tachographs mandatory for all vehicles described in the above section Regulations and manufactured after August 1, 2005. Digital tachographs would be required as of May 1, 2006 for all new vehicles for which EWG regulation VO(EWG)3820/85 applies, as is published in the official newsletter of the European Union L102 from April 11, 2006.

The European Root Certification Authority (ERCA) for the EU's Digital Tachograph has been designed, implemented and is currently operated by the European Commission's Joint Research Centre (JRC) at Ispra, Italy. Tachographs are also useful after an accident to help establish the cause and corroborate eye witness accounts. Trade unions take a dim view of anyone who exceeds speed limits or permitted hours.

Fears that it is easy to falsify readings by tampering with tachographs have been allayed, since it is relatively easy to spot such attempts. Tachograph data, once correlated, provides valuable data to the haulage company. For instance, efficiency of driver and vehicle use, driver shift patterns, compliance with internal policy, payment of agency drivers, proof of collection/delivery times, etc.

If you go to this link on the Internet, you can download free a full government document on current drivers' hours and tachograph rules.

http://www.dft.gov.uk/vosa/repository/Rules%20on%20
Drivers%20Hours%20and%20Tachographs%20-%20Goods%20
vehcles%20in%20the%20UK%20and%20Europe.pdf

APPENDIX 4 - GLOSSARY

-A-

ABS (Antilock Braking System)
Computer, sensors and solenoid valves which together monitor wheel speed and modulate braking force if wheel lockup is sensed during braking. Helps the driver retain control of the vehicle during heavy braking on slippery roads.

AFV (Alternative Fuelled Vehicle)
Vehicle powered by a fuel other than gasoline or diesel.

Air Ride Suspension
Suspension which supports the load on air-filled rubber bags rather than steel springs. Compressed air is supplied by the same engine-driven air compressor and reservoir tanks which provide air to the air brake system.

ATC (Automatic Traction Control)
Usually an optional feature based on ABS, it prevents spinning of the drive wheels under power on sli44ppery surfaces by braking individual wheels and/or reducing engine throttle. Also called ASR, an acronym sometimes loosely translated from the German

as anti-spin regulation.

ATV (All Terrain Vehicle)
Vehicle designed for any type of terrain.

AVI (Automatic Vehicle Identification)
System combining an on-board transponder with roadside receivers to automate identification of vehicles. Uses include electronic toll collection and stolen vehicle detection.

AVL (Automated Vehicle Location)
Class of technologies designed to locate vehicles for fleet management purposes and for stolen vehicle recovery. Infrastructure can be land-based radio towers or satellites.

Axle
* Structural component to which wheels, brakes and suspension are attached.
* Drive axles are those with powered wheels.
* Front axle is usually called the steer axle.
* Pusher axles are unpowered and go ahead of drive axles.
* Rear axles may be drive, tag or pusher types.
* Tag axles are unpowered and go behind drive axles.

-B-

Bill of Lading
Itemised list of goods contained in a shipment.

Blind Spot
Areas around a commercial vehicle that are not visible to the

driver either through the windshield, side windows or mirrors.

Bobtail
Tractor operating without a trailer. Also refers to straight truck.

Bogie
Assembly of two or more axles, usually a pair in tandem.

Brake Horsepower (bhp)
Engine horsepower rating as determined by brake dynamometer testing.

- C -

Cabover (Cab-Over-Engine, COE)
Truck or tractor design in which the cab sits over the engine on the chassis.

Cargo Weight
Combined weight of all loads, gear and supplies on a vehicle.

Cartage Company
Company that provides local (within a town, city or municipality) pick-up and delivery.

Cast Spoke Wheel
Wheel with five or six spokes originating from a centre hub. The spoked portion, usually made of cast steel, is bolted to a multiple-piece steel rim (see Demountable Rim; Disc Wheel).

CB (Citizens Band Radio)
Two-way radio.

CE (CF, LP)
Distance from back of a truck's cab to the end of its frame.

CFC
Chlorofluorocarbon.

CG (Centre of Gravity)
Weight centre or balance point of an object, such as a truck body. Calculated to help determine optimum placement of truck bodies on chassis.

Chassis Weight (Curb Weight, Tare Weight)
Weight of the empty truck, without occupants or load.

CNG
Compressed natural gas.

COE
See Cabover.

Common Carrier
Freight transportation company which serves the general public. May be regular route service (over designated highways on a regular basis) or irregular route (between various points on an unscheduled basis).

Compensated Intracorporate Hauling
Freight transportation service provided by one company for a sister company.

Container (Shipping Container)

Standard-sized rectangular box used to transport freight by ship, rail and highway. International shipping containers are 20 or 40 feet long, conform to International Standards Organization (ISO) standards and are designed to fit in ships' holds.

Container Chassis
Single-purpose semitrailer designed to carry a shipping container.

Contract Carrier
Company that transports freight under contract with one or a limited number of shippers.

Converter Dolly (Dolly)
Auxiliary axle assembly equipped with a fifth wheel (coupling device), towed by a semitrailer and supporting the front of, and towing, another semitrailer.

Cube (Cubic Capacity)
Interior volume of a truck body, semitrailer or trailer, measured in cubic feet.

Curb Weight
See Chassis Weight.

- D -

Dead-Heading
Operating a truck without cargo.

Demountable Rim
Multi-piece steel wheel rim assembly which is bolted to a spoke

hub. Demountable rims are still in use, though they have been replaced in many applications by the simpler disc wheel. (see Cast Spoke Wheel)

Disc Wheel
Single-piece rim/wheel assembly of stamped and welded steel or forged aluminum, anchored by 8 or 10 nuts to a hub.

Displacement (Piston Displacement)
Sum of the volumes swept by an engine's pistons as they travel up and down in their cylinders. Based upon bore (diameter of cylinder) and stroke (distance travelled by piston). Expressed in litres or cubic inches.

Dolly
See Converter Dolly.

Doubles (Twins, Twin Trailers)
Combination of a tractor and two semitrailers connected in tandem by a converter dolly. (see Converter Dolly; Pintle Hook)

Driveline
All the components which together transmit power from the transmission to the drive axle(s). These consist of at least one driveshaft (propeller shaft) with a universal joint at each end.

Drivetrain (Powertrain)
All the components, excluding engine, which transmit the engine's power to the rear wheels: clutch, transmission, driveline and drive axle(s).

DRL (Daytime Running Lights)

System that automatically turns on a vehicle's low beam headlights when the parking brake is released and the ignition is on.

- E -

EDI (Electronic Data Interchange)
The business-to-business interconnection of computers for the rapid exchange of a wide variety of documents, from bills of lading to build tickets at auto plants.

Escape Ramp
See Runaway Truck Ramp.

EV (Electric Vehicle)
Vehicle powered by electric motor(s) rather than by an internal combustion engine. Most common source of electricity is chemical storage batteries.

- F -

Fifth Wheel

Coupling device attached to a tractor or dolly which supports the front of a semitrailer and locks it to the tractor or dolly. The fifth wheel's centre is designed to accept a trailer's kingpin, around which the trailer and tractor or dolly pivot in turns.

Fixed Tandem
Assembly of two axles and suspension that is attached to the

chassis in one place, and cannot be moved fore and aft.

For-Hire Carrier
Company in the business of transporting freight belonging to others (see Private Carrier).

- G -

GAWR (Gross Axle Weight Rating)
Maximum weight an axle is rated to carry by the manufacturer. Includes both the weight of the axle and the portion of a vehicle's weight carried by the axle.

GCW (Gross Combination Weight)
Total weight of a loaded combination vehicle, such as a tractor-semitrailer or truck and full trailer(s).

Geared Speed
Calculated vehicle speed at the engine's governed rpm in each transmission gear, or (commonly) in top gear.

Gear Ratio
Number, usually expressed as a decimal fraction, representing how many turns of the input shaft cause exactly one revolution of the output shaft. Applies to transmissions, power takeoffs, power dividers and rear axles.

Grade
Steepness of a grade, expressed as a percentage.

Gradeability

Vehicle's ability to climb a grade at a given speed. Example: A truck with a gradeability of 5% at 60 mph can maintain 60 mph on a grade with a rise of 5%.

GVW (Gross Vehicle Weight)
Total weight of a vehicle and everything aboard, including its load.

GVWR (Gross Vehicle Weight Rating)
Total weight a vehicle is rated to carry by the manufacturer, including its own weight and the weight of its load.

- H -

Hazmat

Hazardous materials.

Headache Rack

Heavy protective barrier mounted behind the tractor's cab.

HCFC
Hydrochlorofluorocarbon.

Horsepower (hp)
Measure of power (the amount of work that can be done over a given amount of time).

- I -

Independent Trucker
See Owner Operator.

- J -

Jackknife
To place the trailer at a very sharp angle to the tractor.

Jake Brake
See Retarder.

JIT (Just-In-Time)
Manufacturing system which depends on frequent, small deliveries of parts and supplies to keep on-site inventory to a minimum.

- K -

Kingpin (axle)
Pin around which a steer axle's wheels pivot.

Kingpin (trailer)
Anchor pin at the centre of a semitrailer's upper coupler which is captured by the locking jaws of a tractor's fifth wheel to attach the tractor to the semitrailer.

- L -

Landing Gear
Retracting legs which support the front of a semitrailer when it is not coupled to a tractor.

LCV (Long Combination Vehicle)
In general, vehicles longer than a standard doubles rig.

Lessor
Company which leases vehicles.

Lift Axle
Extra, unpowered axle needed only when the vehicle is loaded.

LPG
Liquid propane gas.

Load Range (Tyres)
Letter code system for the weight carrying capacity of tyres.

Low Loader
Open flat-bed trailer with a deck height very low to the ground, used to haul construction equipment or bulky or heavy loads.

- O -

Onboard Computer
See Trip Recorder.

Overdrive
Gearing in which less than one revolution of a transmission's input shaft causes one turn of the output shaft. The purpose of overdrive is to reduce engine rpm in high gear for better fuel economy.

Owner-Operator
Driver who owns and operates his own vehicle.

- P -

P&D
Pickup and delivery.

Payload
Weight of the cargo being hauled.

Pigtail
Cable used to transmit electrical power from the tractor to the trailer. So named because it is coiled like a pig's tail.

Pintle Hook
Coupling device used in double trailer, triple trailer and truck-trailer combinations. It has a curved, fixed towing horn and an upper latch that opens to accept the drawbar eye of a trailer or dolly.

Piston Displacement
See Displacement.

Ply Rating (PR)
Relative measure of tyre casing strength. (see Load Range)

Powertrain
See Drivetrain.

Private Carrier

Business which operates trucks primarily for the purpose of transporting its own products and raw materials. The principle business activity of a private carrier is not transportation.

PSI (Pounds Per Square Inch)
Unit of measurement for tyre air pressure, air brake system pressure and turbocharger boost.

PTO (Power Takeoff)
Device used to transmit engine power to auxiliary equipment. A PTO often drives a hydraulic pump, which can power a dump body, concrete mixer or refuse packer. Some designs mount to a standard opening on the transmission, while others attach at the front or rear of the engine.

Pull Trailer
Short, full trailer (supported by axles front and rear) with an extended tongue.

Pup Trailer
Short semitrailer, usually between 26 and 32 feet long, with a single axle.

Pusher Axle
See Axle.

- R -

Reefer
Refrigerated trailer with insulated walls and a self-powered refrigeration unit. Most commonly used for transporting food.

Retarder
Device used to assist brakes in slowing the vehicle. The most common type of retarder on over-the-road trucks manipulates the engine's valves to create engine drag. (This type is commonly referred to as "Jake Brake" because the predominant manufacturer is Jacobs Vehicle Equipment Co.) Other types of retarders include exhaust retarders, transmission-mounted hydraulic retarders and axle-mounted electromagnetic retarders.

Rolling Radius
Tire dimension from centre of the axle to the ground; measured with tyre loaded to rated capacity. Used in calculating geared speed.

RPM (Revolutions Per Minute)
Measure of the speed at which a shaft spins. Most often used to describe engine crankshaft speed. Indicated by a tachometer.

Runaway Truck Ramp
Emergency area adjacent to a steep downgrade that a heavy truck can steer into after losing braking power. Usually two or three lanes wide and several hundred feet long, the ramp is a soft, gravel-filled pathway which absorbs the truck's forward momentum, bringing it to a safe stop. Depending on the surrounding terrain, the ramp may be level or run up or down hill.

- S -

Semitrailer
Truck trailer supported at the rear by its own wheels and at the front by a fifth wheel mounted to a tractor or dolly.

Single-Source Leasing
Service in which companies can lease drivers and trucks from the same source, rather than having to procure them from different companies.

Sleeper
Sleeping compartment mounted behind a truck cab, sometimes attached to the cab or even designed to be an integral part of it.

Sliding Fifth Wheel
Fifth wheel mounted to a mechanism that allows it to be moved back and forth for the purpose of adjusting the distribution of weight on the tractor's axles. Also provides the capability to vary vehicle combination lengths.

Sliding Tandem (Slider)
Mechanism that allows a tandem axle suspension to be moved back and forth at the rear of a semitrailer, for the purpose of adjusting the distribution of weight between the axles and fifth wheel.

Speedability
Top speed a vehicle can attain as determined by engine power, engine governed speed, gross weight, driveline efficiency, air resistance, grade and load.

Spoke Wheel
See Cast Spoke Wheel.

Straight Truck
See Truck.

SUV
Sport/utility vehicle.

Synchronised Transmission
Transmission with built-in mechanisms to automatically equalise the speed of its gears to allow smooth shifting without the need to double-clutch.

- T -

Tag Axle
See Axle.

Tare Weight
See Chassis Weight.

Tandem Axle (Tandems)
Pair of axles and associated suspension usually located close together.

TEU (Twenty-Foot Equivalent Unit)
Standardised unit for measuring container capacity on ships etc.

Tractor
Truck designed primarily to pull a semitrailer by means of a fifth wheel mounted over the rear axle(s). Sometimes called a truck tractor or highway tractor to differentiate from it from a farm tractor.

Tractor Trailer

Tractor and semitrailer combination.

Tri-Axle
Truck, tractor or trailer with three axles grouped together at the rear. (see Tridem)

Tridem
Group of three axles on a truck, tractor or trailer. Tridems are most common on European semitrailers.

Trip Leasing
Leasing a company's vehicle to another transportation provider for a single trip.

Trip Recorder (On-Board Computer)
Cab-mounted device which electronically or mechanically records data such as truck speed, engine rpm, idle time and other information useful to trucking management.

Truck
Vehicle which carries cargo in a body mounted to its chassis, rather than on a trailer towed by the vehicle.

Twins (Twin Trailers)
See Doubles.

- U -

ULEV
Ultra-low emissions vehicle.

Upper Coupler

Load bearing surface on the underside of the front of a semitrailer. It rests on the fifth wheel of a tractor or dolly and has a downward-protruding kingpin which is captured by the locking jaws of the fifth wheel.

- V -

VIN (Vehicle Identification Number)
Assigned by the manufacturer, this number is unique to each vehicle and appears on the vehicle's registration and title.

- W -

WIM (Weigh-In-Motion)
Technology for determining a vehicle's weight without requiring it to come to a complete stop.